A Biblical Understanding of

Pain

A Biblical Understanding of

Pain

Its Reasons and Realities

JOHN TIMMERMAN

CASCADE *Books* · Eugene, Oregon

A BIBLICAL UNDERSTANDING OF PAIN
Its Reasons and Realities

Cascade Books
An Imprint of Wipf and Stock Publishers
199 W. 8th Ave., Suite 3
Eugene, OR 97401

www.wipfandstock.com

ISBN 13: 978-1-61097-109-6

Cataloging-in-Publication data:

Timmerman, John.

A biblical understanding of pain : its reasons and realities / John Timmerman.

viii + 118 pp. ; 23 cm. Includes bibliographical references.

ISBN 13: 978-1-61097-109-6

1. Suffering—Religious aspects—Christianity. 2. Theodicy. 3. Consolation. I. Title.

BT732.7 T57 2013

Manufactured in the U.S.A.

For Pat
Always with Me

Contents

A Broken Heart

It wasn't a heart attack after all.

And how could it be, I wondered, even as the pain grew in my chest like a succubus. I gasped for breath that I couldn't find. The air left the room and left me sprawled on the living room chair where I normally read the paper, and struggling to breathe.

Thirty years of hard tennis and vigorous racquetball had rendered my knees bony stumps of gristle and shard, but left my heart perking along like a muscular metronome. I had the belated knee replacement scheduled for the following summer. Now I wondered if I would be alive when I arrived at the ER.

Strangely, that thought of dying didn't particularly perturb me. The awful pain did. That succubus had teeth that sank deep into my chest—heart, lungs, and whatever else resides there.

My brain felt numb, as if velvet folds of chloroformed cloth lay there. I was told later my eyes rolled up into my head. I couldn't believe it because a fascinating show of bright flashing orbs danced there, brighter than a thousand stars. They had to come from somewhere. They faded. If only I could breathe.

I have always been claustrophobic and came close to drowning once when I was a boy. Then I had a similar feeling, and a resigned reaction—well, this is it. But I'll fight back a little more.

And then I don't have to, of course. The ambulance arrives; the efficient EMTs enact their ministrations. I succumb. I don't have to fight, only endure. The thought crosses my mind: when does endurance become dying?

Anything to stop the pain that has settled over my torso like a chain coat, inside the flesh, in the land of hurt. The hospital is not far away, and too far. The EMT has slipped six nitroglycerin tablets under my tongue by the time we arrive.

Heart patients get the express lane. The gurney wheels through corridors to our own little, sterile monastery where we huddle like flagellated monks. Nurses hoist my ungainly bulk from the gurney to a bed. By now I am hypomanic with the pain meds and nitroglycerin. I crack jokes and make puns with the attending physician as she fastens wires and bends across my torso.

"Tune in a different channel, Doc. I don't like the heavy rock on that one."

"Ah, yes. Golden oldies for the old boy. That's more like it."

The bewildered cardiologist turns to my wife. "Is he himself?" she asks.

Sadly, I think, my wife answers, "Yes."

I burst out in hysterical laughter. "Myself," I say. "Been looking for that rascal all my life."

Finally the pills do what they're supposed to—induce a drunken, deathlike sleep. I am aware of flashing light now and then, machinery clicking.

The next morning I am wheelchaired to tests. I am helped out of the wheelchair to clamber onto a treadmill. I collapse in seconds. "Well, that was fun," I tell the doctor, a new one, of course. Probably specialized in the treadmill to nowhere, the existential highway. Myself isn't. They trundle me onto a bed and inject dobutamine. Artificial exercise. Within seconds my heartbeat is pounding a kettle drum in my ears, my scalp lifts slightly.

No abnormalities, really. Except it's hard to draw a breath. Drowned people have that problem too. So let's try more tests.

A heart catheter is run from my crotch into my heart. A little man in there with a miniature camera must take the pictures. Everything's fine in all the rooms of that heart. Living proof.

So my heart is good. I have the certified stamp of approval. I have already signed away my organs for donation upon my death. Here is a good one to harvest—a Cadillac of hearts, lots of miles left. Just give it to someone else who needs it more than I will reposing in the moldy grave; I'll probably get a new one in heaven. I might not need one at all.

But now I've been on the costly heart unit for two days and these doctors, these circling non-entities, aren't satisfied. Clearly something is amiss. Here rational deduction intrudes. What else lies in that old thoracic cavity? A set of lungs, of course.

That evening my daughter brought my five-year-old grandson, Logan, to see me. Logan and I share one of those special relationships that only grandpas—or "Papa" in his vocabulary—are privileged to have. It's called "rough-housing" and "tickle-treatment." Every Monday since he was an infant, grandma and grandpa have had this young dynamo, this flurry of arms and legs, this smooth dark skin, these perfect brown eyes, in our possession. Our time ends after a restaurant dinner or when he falls asleep.

And why shouldn't he sleep. The rough-housing is wild, pure abandonment to frolic. He lies in wait for me when I get home from work, sneaks up on me when I'm changing clothes (I know where you are every second, Logan), emerges with a shriek. We tumble and roll across the once neat bed. We storm down to the living room, play bucking bronco or hide and seek until we both collapse on the floor, utterly spent but still giggling like a pair of cubs, hardly human in our glee.

Tonight he stands uncertainly by my daughter, holding her hand, half hiding behind her.

Yes, I think. A hospital is a confounding place, isn't it, dear grandson? These beds were not made for frolic.

A tear slips his eye, a silvery track down the brown cheek.

My daughter asks, "Don't you want to give Papa a hug?"

He shakes his head slowly. The voice is soft, so very soft the words float, "I don't want to break Papa's heart," he said.

Oh, my child. So this is your torment. Did you really think that all our wild love-frolic broke Papa's heart? So you took it upon your own thin shoulders.

Forgive me, dear child. Forgive my blindness.

I called him to the bedside, ran my hand across his tight curls, wiped away the tear with my index finger, held his hand. He raised those wise brown eyes. "Logan, Papa's heart is just fine. You'll be able to rough-house with Papa all you want."

He didn't fully believe me, of course. Fear is never easily erased. But at least I spoke honestly. Tomorrow they would do the excavation of my lungs.

The sedatives again. I wonder if I'm myself, living in this dopey dream world of pharmaceuticals. A pulmonologist had studied the cat-scan or MRI or a Ouija board and detected some warty growths residing like a fungal forest in the bottom of my left lung. These he would excise—I no longer cared how—and test for malignancy. Well, I thought, what a rotten way to go. But by then I was on my way to sleep and only dimly aware of a small tube threading up my nostril.

Another night on the flat cold bed, waiting for results. It wasn't cancer. Benign. Probably some deposits from some long ago pneumonia embedded like dirty tailings in the lung tissue. I was sent home—along with follow-up appointments with the pulmonologists.

But what was the problem? Why was it that when I had to climb twenty-two stairs from my first floor classroom to my second floor office, I had to stop at every landing to catch my breath? And why, when I reached the top, dizzy and reeling with black spots and white lights in my eyes, did I have to lean against the wall before getting sufficient balance to make it to my office? Maybe not just Papa's heart but his whole body was broken.

Repeated tests later my lung capacity was finally pronounced normal. If this was normal, if I had to snail-creep my way around hallways, take elevators instead of steps, have a colleague carry my briefcase when it was too heavy, then, I thought, it wasn't much to my liking. In fact, it was pretty nearly pointless.

It just so happened that about that time I had my semi-annual medication check with a psychiatrist, whose wisdom and grace lent as much balance to my life as did the medications. I related my symptoms to him, telling also of my frustration with the fact that, after countless tests, these white-coated technocrats had found no identifiable cause. He listened, nodded, then thought a moment. "I know exactly what it is," he said. "And I can tell you how to get better."

He turned to the computer and printed out six pages from the Mayo Clinic website diagnostic manual. "Here," he said. "Tell me if these sound familiar." I read them one by one, placing a mental check mark by each. If there were such a thing as a diagnostic grid, I fit perfectly. Scored 100 percent at my very first test: Metabolic Syndrome.

"Sounds almost too easy," I observed.

"It isn't. Most doctors today are trained to do tests in a specialized area. Sometimes the hard part is seeing the whole picture. The hard part for you is what you're going to have to do about it."

I groaned. There's always a catch.

"First, I want you to lose thirty pounds."

"I don't have it to lose."

"Yes. You do. You're a large man so you carry it well. Think about this. Two of the medications I prescribe contribute to weight gain."

Well, I knew that. "Can we change the meds?"

He shook his head. "Not wise. They're doing very well what they're supposed to do." He turned and scrawled some figures on paper. "Here's your daily limits for carbs, calories, and cholesterol."

I studied the sheet. "This is less than my dog gets."

He nodded. "You'll have to make friends with hunger."

I have enough friends, thank you.

"Make no mistake," he added. "This is a deadly syndrome. You also have to start some low impact exercise—walk as much as your bones permit, ride a bicycle."

I wouldn't say the pounds melted off, but six months later I had lost thirty-five of them. True, my "large" body looked like a shadow of itself. When I flexed my biceps they looked like a couple of dimes standing on edge. My legs looked like legs instead of sausages. Best of all, I could walk the dog around the block without feeling like I would collapse. I could do chores around the house—and finish them.

No, that's not best of all. Logan still comes over every Monday. He hides when his Papa comes home from work. Then he barrels out of his hiding place and is all over me, rolling on the floor, playing bucking bronco, getting a tickle treatment.

And all things are made glad in my heart.

But not quite all, for I have this to consider. Oddly, during the pain and tests, I thought of Jesus. Not that this is an infrequent matter, but this was different. I did not think of Jesus as the standby friend, nor as a cosmic comforter, although I would have taken either one at the time. No, with a physiology and metabolism apparently as unusual as mine, I thought of Jesus's heart.

I am told that Jesus suffocated.

Nailed as he was to the patibulum and post, nailed through ankles and wrists, Jesus had to push himself up against the nails to draw a breath. As his strength failed, his lungs began to fill with fluids. Simultaneously, unable to breathe except by increasingly futile gasps, his pericardium filled with serous fluids. Some call it suffocation by drowning.

I am told it was a Latin cross, the *crux immissa*, since the superscription was fixed above his head. The King of the Jews. Blood flowed copiously from the thorn-induced scalp wounds, the torn flesh of the flagellum, the ruptured wrists and ankles. But loss of blood did not kill him. He was dead by the time the soldiers came to break his legs and end the ugly spectacle.

I wonder about that one reckless soldier. Was he frightened beyond belief? Did a blood lust seize him? He strode to the dead figure and rammed his spear into its side. As he pierced lungs and pericardium, blood and water flowed from the wound. The Living Water. My blood shed for you.

Truly, Jesus died of suffocation. I believe the medical autopsy.

And I believe, with every beat of my own curious heart, that Jesus died of a broken heart.

So it is; so it was; so it shall forever be.

This is not a matter of clinical certainty, but of belief. And it seems to me yet today that in matters of pain we are still caught between those two poles—the clinical and the experience.

When one is too certain about God, when one always has the right pieces in a theological puzzle, when one always knows the answers to the problems of others, then it is very likely that one believes more in dogma than in God.

The history of humanity since Eden has been one of pressing toward knowledge and certainty about God. As God made clear in the prophecies of Isaiah, however, "My thoughts are not your thoughts, neither are your ways my ways" (Isa 55:8). Our longing for certainty tends to falter in clouds of unknowing.

That same central theme is the heart of God's discourse with Job (chapters 38–41). Job is positioned as many of us are. Blinded by pain, we seek immediate answers from a God whose ways are not our ways, nor whose thoughts are our thoughts. Because of that, we grow suspicious when human answers come too glibly, uncolored by human experience or spiritual struggle. We look instead for answers that come from some source beyond human experience, some source with ultimate authority.

As we press on to certainty about God, we discover that God has given much by which to know him. The Bible itself illuminates the great sweep of human history under God, how he interacts with us, loves us, sets standards for right behavior for us. God has given us his Son, the central event in human history whereby we glimpse our eternal destiny. God has given his Holy Spirit to guide us toward that destiny, to give us the breath of life, to empower and enable us. All this so we can know God better.

But not perfectly, for we have spots in our eyes. They get there each time we turn from God's way to our way. They get there through sin. Moreover, we are born with them, and they darken throughout our lives. Some people may give up, choosing to live in the shadows. Some press on even when sight grows cloudy.

"Now," wrote St. Paul, "we see but a poor reflection as in a mirror" (1 Cor 13:12). The first-century mirror of Paul's time was nothing like the piercing clarity of our time. It was simply a dull, cloudy piece of polished metal. To probe the reality of our limited human knowing of God, other versions change the metaphor slightly. For example, the King James Version renders it: "For now we see through a glass darkly."

The metaphor Paul uses, however, still applies perfectly. Our spiritual vision is clouded by sin. Because of sin, we cannot know God, nor his plan for our lives, perfectly. To claim to do so is an act of arrogance, a kind of self-idolatry.

But why should we want to do so? God is wrapped in majesty, the fires of his beauty and holiness so powerful humans cannot look upon him. Moreover, God is cloaked in mystery. He is the Creator; we his creation. He is omnipotent; our power shrivels at the slightest threat. He is all-knowing; however mysteriously he has made us, it's no mystery that our knowledge is limited. The list of God's great and infinite qualities could be extended nearly to infinity itself when compared to our mere finitude.

Yet, when we suffer pain, when the course of our lives is rudely or tragically interrupted, we call on God for understanding. At such times we might wonder why this gulf between God and us is so great. Sometimes, we feel abandoned by God altogether. On this side of the great divide, in this sin-sickened world, the pain of our suffering is acute. Sometimes we wonder if that great divide to the mysterious God, the one we can only know in part as if through a cloudy glass, has any bridge whatsoever. Or, are we abandoned to affliction, without hope of divine grace here and now? Does the cloud on the mirror prevent us from ever seeing clearly—until we cross the great divide from this life into the next?

With so many questions and so little certitude, it seems reasonable to assert that we humans cannot understand pain in our lives without understanding the God who has made us. We press on toward certitude, but final answers seem to lie beyond the pale of our knowing and come instead from a divine source.

What kind of answers might we find, when, prompted by pain, we look to God for direction? What knowledge and comfort can we discover?

Although the Bible reveals to us many traits of God, by which we both know him and understand the ways we can't know him fully in this life,

God himself has sent his divine mediator Jesus, who, while we can know him fully as our human Redeemer, is also at once God himself. And although with a certainty sin has clouded our human understanding, we can with equal certainty testify that Jesus, who loves us to and beyond the cross, has certain answers to the pain that bewilders us. That is the subject of this book—to understand the bewildering presence of pain in our lives and to find those spiritual truths that speak directly to our bewilderment. That is the first and essential answer we need.

To do this, we have to be honest with the problem of pain itself. It is not a figment of our imagination; it drops hot coals into our lives and burns into every tissue of our being. Pain hurts. Pain is an X-rated scream of terror. And always pain affects us as whole persons: physically, psychologically, emotionally, and, most certainly, spiritually. Basically, we have to understand who we are that need God's answers. To fail to do this, to fail to be honest with ourselves, is something like a person who has a few drinks before going to an AA meeting. He or she has just plain missed the point.

One of the negative effects of what we call contemporary postmodernism—the belief that we live strictly for ourselves, that no spiritual or divine presence exists, and that we are simply subject to natural laws—is the thorough diminishment of human nature. Basically, in this view you and I and all other humans are just corks tossed around on the sea of life. We do have desires, however, so one of our aims is to live in such a way that these desires are met. Whoever gets the most toys before dying wins. This is the majority world and life view today, sad to say.

Postmodernism carries a host of problems in a dirty sack over its shoulders, however. In denying God, it denies too much of what it means to be human, especially what we call the "desire for God." Furthermore, it denies our ethical nature. Our sense of right and wrong is replaced with "relativism" or tolerance for any point of view as long as it doesn't interfere with mine. So we also lose any sense of social justice. We lose our emotional selves. The "fire within" that seeks God is replaced by a fire to satisfy our own desires. And what right do I have to do this? Here the great slogan of postmodernism: "If it feels good, do it."

A Christian worldview disagrees with this prevalent declaration that my needs are more important than any other needs, including those God has placed upon us. Especially in the experience of pain. God has told us to "Love the Lord your God with all your heart and with all your soul and with all your mind and with all your strength" (Luke 12:30). God has created us as whole persons, with one purpose: to love God and our neighbors as ourselves.

Two implications arise from this when we suffer pain. First, we suffer as whole persons. Our strength (physical), soul (relational to God), heart (emotional), and mind (intellectual) are involved in the experience of pain. Second, we need answers that sufficiently touch each area if we are ever to comprehend the role of pain in the Christian life.

We also understand, however, that pain does not have the last word on this earth. It is not all powerful; only God is. God sets the limits; he sets the boundaries when our pain-riven lives don't even know if there are boundaries, when we wonder how we can possibly go on.

Just hours before his arrest, and fully aware of his own suffering on the cross, Jesus prayed some of the most tender words imaginable with his disciples. He will not leave them as orphans, he says (John 14:18). These believers are his children. Never will they be separated from the love of God.

Then, in a passage that breaks one's heart, so tender it is, Jesus promises: "Peace I leave with you; my peace I give to you. I do not give as the world gives. Do not let your hearts be troubled and do not be afraid" (John 14:27). Into our pain Jesus speaks peace. Against that peace the power of sin and pain cannot stand.

We want to consider the full picture of pain, then. We want to examine why we suffer pain and what role sin bears upon it. We want, secondly, to understand how pain affects us as whole persons. Finally, we want to examine the biblically-based answers that respond to the myriad of questions arising from the experience of pain. Perhaps, in that undertaking we can find some measure of the peace that Jesus has assured us.

Chapter One

"I Don't Need Any Help"

The Denial of Pain

THIS BOOK STARTED IN a rather ordinary way. Having endured a series of blows in our own and in our extended family, my wife and I began to ponder the why of pain. Isn't that always the way? Pain creeps into our lives on padded little feet or with claws extended, sometimes leaping in, but always at the least expected moment. Life goes its accustomed way, then suddenly pain is there, howling its piercing cry.

When Pat and I reflected on the why of the pain we were experiencing, we had no wish at first to define it. Even less did we want to understand it, to bend the mind against its unyielding surface and say, yes, here is where the pain started. We wanted it gone. We understood only that we hurt, and we wondered why.

Pain is not a bacterium under a laboratory microscope that you can label and devise some quick treatment plan for it. Pain burrows into us, leaving a trail of bewilderment.

If anything, pain is worsened by the fact that there are so few ready answers. Pain drives us inward. One of its most sinister effects is isolation. Writing in *The Christian Century*, Kathryn Greene-McCreight observes that "Sufferers are isolated from those around them by the very fact of their pain, which creates a burden of suffering distinct from the pain itself."[1] Similarly, in "After Great Pain," Joan D. Chittister argues that struggle is a very private thing. Consequently, "It happens to the very depths of our souls."[2] This, writes Chittister, creates the deep sense of isolation, and also, therefore, the mysterious complexity of pain.

1. Greene-McCreight, "Review of Three Books," 39.
2. Chittister, "After Great Pain," 38.

If pain varies from person to person depending upon its source, the consequence is always that the individual person endures the full effect of that pain in his or her own individual way. No one else, as in some great chess game, shuffles across the board at some strategic moment, enters into you, and endures the pain for you. Others may support you, but you carry it alone. Isolation turns us inward; it shrinks us to that malevolent thing that has burrowed into your life.

If you have ever had that sense of shrunken isolation, where pain has taken over your life and not left much else, then you too have breathed that word why. When isolation cuts that deeply, we either give in to it, or we seek the help of others. But the great mystery to me is this: why do so many people deny the presence of pain altogether? Why do they refuse to seek help? Why do they think you should try to fight through it? Several answers spring to mind, but they strike me as offshoots of three main branches.

Beauty from Ashes

Before we tackle the central issue, we might benefit by glancing at a rather odd view that lies right between acknowledging our individual pain and the denial of pain. As I began seeking answers to the why of pain that won't just go away, I began to scour dozens of books and articles on the topic. These were by Christian and non-Christian authors alike. I confess that I cringed at several of them.

One author wrote of the "gift" of different kinds of pain—from cancer to depression. Another wrote of the "joy" and "blessings" of suffering. Still another told me to "embrace my pain." I would rather hug a porcupine. It will make me a stronger person, the writer advised. I never wanted to be Hercules, thank you. I don't want to embrace my pain; I want to get rid of it.

Yet, we also admit that in some strange way suffering can produce rare and lasting beauty. Consider, for example, the pain-ridden life of Johann Sebastian Bach (1685–1750). His parents died within eight months of each other, leaving him an orphan at age ten. After training on the organ, Bach married his second cousin, Maria Barbara Bach. When Barbara gave birth to twins, Bach thought this the greatest and dearest gift a husband could receive. It struck him that the saddest blow a man could receive, then, would be the loss of a child's life. He was not prepared for what would happen.

Returning from a two-month vacation at the Carlsbad Spas in Bohemia (now a state of Czechoslovakia), Bach walked toward his front door and noticed a black wreath hanging there. His heart melted. It wasn't one of the twins, however. His beloved wife, Barbara, had died. In the music he wrote during the following months, in the violin partitas and cello suites, one can hear the voice of pain. Grief seeps through each note.

In an article on what artists do with pain, Ruth Ann Ridley wrote: "They make something of their sufferings. Bach's music we turn to when our lives have become intolerably chaotic and we yearn to hear resolution. It is music both tinged with pain and pulsing with life. It is rich with the feeling of love."[3] Many Christians feel they move in and out of the same shadowed world that Bach did, trying to make some music out of their pain. Can one find any harmony in the effort? Often it seems that all the notes are discordant.

Bach suffered personally. He fathered twenty children with Barbara and his second wife, Anna Magdalena, only seven of whom survived his lifetime. Moreover, he met with concerted opposition or mere indifference to his music during his lifetime. In his elder years his vision deteriorated. Seeking treatment in Leipzig, he submitted to eye surgery, during which he died. One wonders how someone who endured such a disharmonious life could create such lush harmonies in his work.

Bach is an example of beauty that might emanate from suffering. Nearly 1,000 of his works survive him. We could probably name many more artists who suffered terribly and yet produced great and lasting work. It is a bit different, though, to witness beauty arising from suffering, than to say that we are to embrace the suffering itself.

Nonetheless, these writings on pain as a joy or a blessing or something sent to teach us a lesson bother me. I have never believed pain was a gift. I have never believed suffering is cause for joy. (The famous passage of James 1:2 speaks to another matter altogether.) Pain, by definition, hurts. Therefore, I kneel at the mourner's bench, wondering why.

Many others kneel there with me, in an endless row, minds baffled and hearts sinking to the floor. Bewilderment surfaces through a sea of hurt.

Furthermore, I believe we commit a grave theological error if we deny the reality of our pain. If we do, we also deny the rupture in our nature from image of God to fallen humanity. If we deny that, we deny our need. If we deny our need we deny our Savior and the pain he suffered to save us. Consider the theological facts of Jesus's crucifixion.

3. Ridley, "From Chaos to Cosmos," 7.

Jesus endured evil on the cross. Indeed, in that act he suffered pain unimaginable. But the curse of the cross and the victory of the cross are twined together in an ultimate triumph over the cause, the root cause, of pain itself. That is evil. As long as we dwell on this earth, we will not escape suffering. While many of our choices and actions visit the penalty of pain upon us (witness a drug addict in detox), it simply will not do to say that because Jesus suffered, we shouldn't. What Jesus did in his pain was to take the penalty of our sin upon himself and to remove the sting of death. As N. T. Wright points out in his book *Evil and the Problem of Justice*, Jesus's sacrifice on the cross was indeed an atonement theology (he took my sin upon him) and stood in my place as the sacrifice. But it is also a Christus Victor theme where "Jesus has won the victory over the powers of evil."[4] Yet, in several peculiar ways, many people today live in convicted denial of pain or a refusal to acknowledge the presence of pain. To understand this is almost as puzzling as understanding the why of pain itself. As we consider different ways in which people deny the reality of pain, each of us can very likely find persons who readily fit each category. Sometimes they are ourselves.

The Analgesic of Clichés

Perhaps because of simple ignorance, many people deny the reality of pain through the ready-made world of clichés. A cliché is simply a trite or overused expression that essentially does not mean anything. That doesn't prevent their use. They have insinuated their way into popular culture and our everyday language. When they are applied like some balm to suffering, however, they degrade the experience of pain itself. Rather than helping, they accentuate the experience. It's like spreading butter on a third degree burn.

My wife and I were the so-called "surprised" parents. I suppose we had always been so; God seemed to turn up one delightful twist after another just to keep us a bit off balance and trusting him. We had thought, at first, that we couldn't conceive. After all the tests and fertility experts over the course of six years, we gladly decided to adopt. Nine months after our adoption application, we held a baby son in our arms. Maybe that opened the door (so to speak), since thirteen months later Pat gave birth to our first daughter. And a few years later to our second daughter. There was nothing of our design in this. We just rejoiced.

---

4. Wright, *Evil and the Problem of Justice*, 95.

The fact was that we were also moving along in years. We thought this was the last. We were entirely content with that thought. The quiver, as the Bible has it, was sufficiently full. I would watch these three energetic kids roar around the park across the street and murmur, "My cup runneth over." There was, however, just a bit left.

I'll never forget the day Pat showed me the pregnancy test. Call me dumb, but I stared and finally croaked, "What does that mean?" What it meant was that I was going to be a daddy in my dotage.

But this one was different. Oh, our baby boy was born as healthy as could be, with a set of lungs that shook all six floors of the hospital. "This ain't no Cabbage Patch doll," the doctor observed. But it wasn't routine for Pat. Several weeks later she fell into a profound, incapacitating postpartum depression—that illness attributed to the wild, roller-coaster ride of hormones that constitutes childbirth. She required nearly seven weeks of intense hospitalization, and the failure of several pharmaceutical approaches, to regain enough strength to rejoin the family. Regain, in this case, was relative. It took several years for her to overcome the full effects of the devastating toll of depression.

Thus it was a glad day for us when we were first able to go to church as a family. We rejoined our larger family who had lovingly sustained us with prayer, meals, and occasional childcare. Yet, as we were leaving church, one well-intentioned soul bustled toward Pat and asked, "Now, Pat. What really was the problem?" I felt like giving her a lecture on the hormonal system and brain receptors.

I suppose one could call this "denial out of ignorance." Depression is still a baffling and vague term for many moderns. It's easier to say, "I broke my leg." But it is symptomatic of a method by which we moderns deal with pain. "Just lift yourself up by your bootstraps (whatever they are)." "Be a real man." "Grin and bear it." And, of course, "Others have it much worse." These are clichés. They deny the reality of pain.

This, however, is my pain. I own it. No one else is enduring it. But then, well-meaning Christians might respond, "Jesus endured it all on the cross." And one wants to shout: "I am not Jesus." The very thought plunges one headlong into shame and guilt. Into isolation.

Finally, that is the effect of clichés. Since they mean little or nothing, they further reduce the person suffering pain to isolation. They effectively deny the reality and ferocity of pain.

At their base level, clichés are little linguistic pebbles of deceit. They compromise; they hedge; they duck the truth. They are the paintball players of language, ducking through a maze of words until they wound someone.

Contrary to the glib use of clichés, our first lesson in understanding pain, then, is that we have to dignify our pain by acknowledging its reality. I hurt, must be our confession before help can arrive. As the next form of denial makes clear, it is something of a cruel honesty, for it makes us very, very vulnerable.

The Will to Power

In our age, people have nearly obliterated God from human life. But when one ignores God, one has to fill that void with something else. Usually the choice is oneself—"I'll just live for myself"—or some other powerful figure drawn from politics or business or whatever else stands close at hand. The powerful, simply by virtue of having power, have no moral obligation to address the needs or pain of those without power. The effects of this modern rage for power are twofold.

The first effect is all too common—a reluctance or refusal to admit to personal pain. We live in the age of the stiff upper lip and the glamorized public face. Far be it from those who cherish power to show a twitch in those stoic lips or even the thinnest crack in the public image. We are in control. We hide things.

If the first effect is to deny personal pain in ourselves (big boys and girls, and especially powerful ones, don't cry), the second is then to avoid the presence of pain in others. We tend to be reluctant to enter those areas of our society where suffering is most evident. We're uncomfortable with less than fortunate people. It may be dangerous; it may pop the balloon of comfort around our own lives. The American poet Gwendolyn Brooks wrote a poem, "Lovers of the Poor," that brings this fear of others into startling clarity. In her poem, a group of very wealthy, north-side Chicago women are at their guild meeting and decide to do something for the poor. On the assigned day they arrive at a squalid tenement house to deliver their gifts. Appalled by the filth and stench, they turn and run, convinced that it would be preferable to drop their gifts in the mail.

Another variation on the theme of power and pain, however, surfaces in a peculiar and dangerous way. In our society, and even in many of our churches, a feeling prevails that pain is somehow unseemly. It disrupts things. I find this especially so in the carefully scripted liturgies of modern churches. Pain is disruptive. It skewers the neat equilibrium of our lives. So we hide it before those whose lives seem so orderly.

A student walked into my office late on a winter day. "I hope I'm not interrupting," she said.

I have two policies when I talk to students. I blank the computer screen and don't answer the phone.

I invited her in. One glance told me her state. I've seen it countless times.

"I hurt," she said. "And I don't know where to go."

After listening a long time, and arranging professional help for her, I was haunted by the words: "I hurt. And I don't know where to go."

It's no surprise they echoed. I remembered that chilly Sunday morning when Mary ran to the tomb. Two angels appeared and asked, "Woman, why are you crying?"

Mary's words still ring across the centuries. "They have taken my Lord away, and I don't know where they have put him" (John 20:13). Mary was in pain, she hurt, and she didn't know where to go.

So many Marys dwell among us—and Jacks, and Dannys, and Bills. Mary, and the young woman who came to my office that winter day, dared to name their pain. "I hurt." "They have taken my Lord away." These are pleas of the frantic mind, made so by suffering acute loss and pain. But do we dare make that announcement in our own modern churches? To whom? Where? When? Do we dare intrude? Will others think our pain is something easily dismissible, as of no account?

Salvation Through Technology

We moderns also deny the reality of pain by placing our hope in rational, technological science. No one will deny the powerful advances that medical technology has brought to alleviate pain. Intricate surgeries are performed today that were unheard of as little as twenty years ago. New pharmaceuticals counter the menace of pain in our bodies. Yet, many take technology to the level of freeing humanity of pain, indeed, of perfecting humanity. When the knees wear out to the point where bone grinds against bone (as mine did), one can get a new set of knees implanted or medications to ease the pain. Yet, what we tend to forget is that pain precedes the application of the technology, that the technology doesn't work in all cases, and that tragedy which no technology can touch continues to plague our humanity. We still suffer pain.

It is an idea as old as the eighteenth century, really. The Very Important People of society then were the rational thinkers. In fact, they placed their own minds in place of God by relegating God to some distant stretch of the cosmos. This is called Deism. God has no practical intervention in their lives; therefore, it was their task, through rational invention, to save themselves. So it was that technology began walking through the centuries, one invention upon another, until it arrived at the blistering pace of the modern age. So why not place your salvation in science? Look what it has done with amazing cures and alleviations. We have no need for miracles from God; we have the miracle of modern science. So goes the thinking.

One of the most disquieting books of the latter half of the twentieth century is *Walden Two*, whose author, the behavioral scientist B. F. Skinner, investigates a humanity engineered by science. At its climax, the text argues that the behaviorist provides salvation for humanity, that he in fact replaces God:

"It must be a great satisfaction," I said finally. "A world of your own making."

"Yes," he [Frazier] said, "I look upon my work and, behold, it is good."[5] The narrator is struck incredulous—and nearly speechless—by the biblical echo.

He presses Frazier further, whereupon Frazier points out that he has done a better job of it than God. "God's children," he points out, "are always disappointing him."[6] There is no danger of that in *Walden Two*, for everyone has been behaviorally programmed to perform in one way. Worse, they are programmed to believe they are completely free to choose that way: "Their behavior is determined, yet they're free."[7]

Before we complain too loudly about the burden of free will or the unfairness of divine will, this is the alternative. It is essentially a world without emotion or meaning, save for those dictated by the engineers. At one point Frazier observes, "What is love . . . except another name for the use of positive reinforcement."[8]

5. Skinner, *Walden Two*, 295.
6. Ibid., 296.
7. Ibid., 297.
8. Ibid., 300.

A world run by science, directed by the rules of some super-elitist technocrats, is a sterile world. Like a cubed room with its sides painted blank white, it is no place for humanity to pick up its abode.

Truly, medical discoveries have brought relief from pain and health from disease. Where would we be without insulin, polio vaccines, and antibiotics? But there is another way to look at all this—that is, God has gifted certain humans to these discoveries, whether those humans are aware of it or not. We call this God's love, mercy, and grace for a fallen people. And God, as one old hymn has it, "is the ruler yet" ("This is My Father's World").

Taken together these three forms of denial, among others, govern the lives of many "normal" people. It isn't exactly that they are ignorant of pain, although that may factor in. Rather, they have tried to blind themselves to the presence of pain. The problem, then, rests in the fact that the denial is a lie; it can't be done. We lose too much of reality by escaping to a comfort world of clichés, of denial through power, and complete reliance upon technology.

He was once one of the most brilliant men I have known. And a terrific baseball player whose blazing throw from short to first seemed to leave a trail of sparks. By human standards, I guess that he didn't deserve that long, slow slide into death, like an engine that grinds out after too many miles. He had wanted to die years before, feeling that life had no more reasonable place for him. His memory played tricks on him as the brain slipped toward Alzheimer's. Although, a few months before he died, I read the Bible to him—Romans 8—and he commented, "That's world class literature." He laughed. We always prayed with him before leaving. On that day he recited the Lord's Prayer in High German, the language his father had preached in ninety-five years earlier. They were the last comprehensible words I ever heard, replaced thereafter by a confusing and inaccessible rattle of sounds. That was the reality, not a cliché. My father was powerless over the most menial elements of self care.

And that athlete's body? So many bones had broken one loses count. Hips, arms, shoulders, fingers. All the technology in the world couldn't knit him back together again.

We visited him regularly, even when we didn't know if he was aware of our presence. My wife and sister were there when the labored breathing ceased. They saw him die, but they also saw pain release its hold upon him. Never again will it touch him.

Pain cannot be denied, glossed over, reduced to clichés, or dissipated by rational technology. If we have joy in the midst of suffering, there are still pieces of glass in that joy. Joy doesn't cover up or blot out the pain like some great cosmic swash of white-out.

I come full circle to my first question, the enduring question, why? I can't find myself in one of these three camps by which many modern people deny the presence and urgency of pain. Maybe their philosophies give them comfort, even as they live in a hardened shell of denial. But sometimes the cry of pain is a harsh scream, the obliteration of tears in a waiting room, the silent nighttime watch as one awaits the return of a wayward child, the trembling in one's hands as fear drives pellets of ice into the heart.

What is it that does this? Who is the fearful enemy? What do people mean when they talk about pain, anyway? Is it a hangnail or a heroin addiction? After discussing ways by which people try to deny the reality of pain, let's undertake the difficult task of defining pain itself.

Chapter Two

_____

Where on Earth Does Pain Come From?

I HEARD GEORGIA PREACH last night.

My, but she was a regal woman. A large woman, her silk, leopard-skin patterned dress flowed about her. Rings adorned every finger and three toes protruding from her ivory sandals. Ropes of gold chain hung about her neck. Inch-long fingernails were adorned with several hues of polish.

And Georgia could preach.

No, she didn't stamp and stride around the crowded room. She sat in the same metal folding chair as everyone else, except that her dress billowed and swished like a silken cloud.

The chairs were arranged in circles—for family and friends and the addicts here in the recovery house. Every sort of addict was there—heroin, alcohol, cocaine, and others—in this place where they hoped to take the first steps out of the abyss. Georgia had come to support her boyfriend, now entering his fifth week of recovery.

And why should Georgia preach? She knew, from the inside out, and any time someone knows it that way, it has the raw force of truth. That's why Georgia preached. She was one of them, there in the circle.

"Some people are going to tell you," she said, "that you've got to find the root of the problem. That's not so. You got to find the seed!"

In her thirty-two years as an addict, and through her failed attempts at recovery, Georgia, who has been sober now for twelve years, thought she found plenty of roots. She was a violent young woman, full of rage. At the age of nine she went after a schoolmate with a razor—the first in a long series of conflicts with the law.

Drugs and alcohol helped her escape her own violence. But these addictions deepened and grew more expensive. The easiest way to make money was to walk the streets. "I was a pretty girl. Even then when I was killing myself," she says matter-of-factly.

Georgia preached the truth.

"That anger wasn't the root of my problem," she said. "It wasn't the seed, either. It took me a long time to discover. One root was that my cousin started abusing me when I was three years old. That's where the root grew.

"But the real seed of the problem was me. I felt I was in control. Even when crack cocaine had its fingers around my neck and was squeezing down hard, even when I had no life left, I felt I was in control."

That last word rang in the crowded room.

"I had to deny the power of drugs and believe I had power over them, even when I was lying and thieving, to pretend I had control. And now this is hard. When you're pretending you have power and you're really powerless, you ain't nothing.

"Know what I was? I was a body owned by alcohol and drugs. I didn't have no mind left, no soul."

Some people in the group nodded.

"I wasn't no more than a worm lying on the sidewalk. Know what's gonna happen?" she said.

"You'll get stepped on," a tall, thin man said. His hands trembled, making the long snake tattoos up each arm come alive.

"You'll get squished!" Georgia said. "Because I hadn't found the real seed of my problem. I denied I had a problem. I was in control! The real seed was that I needed to admit that. I needed someone to lift the load. I needed to set aside my own self. I needed Jesus."

A long quiet.

"I'm here to tell you," Georgia said. "It's every day in your life as long you have life that you got to remember that. You can't do it yourself. You don't have the control or power. Twelve years sober and I tell Jesus that every day. I talked with him this morning on it."

"No sir," she added, "Ain't no pain that Jesus can't answer as long as you tell him about it. Say, I can't do this on my own. I need help. And there ain't no pain Jesus can answer if you deny it. Say, I'm in control here."

The tall thin man ran his hand over a head shaved bald. "My mama had a saying," he said. His voice was soft, almost shy. "Jesus, he don't always come just when we want him to, but he always comes just at the right time."

Pain and Evil in the Historical Christian Tradition

Throughout history, as long as they have suffered pain, people have grappled with the presence of evil. In fact, many ancient religions would invoke whole pantheons of gods through sacrifices to deter some great evil occurring on earth. In many of these religions, humans were viewed as victims caught in great cosmic battles between dueling gods.

Most of these ancient religions had very little sense of what constituted evil. Like all people, however, adherents knew what constituted pain. Pain came when you were hungry. So they made sacrifices, often blood sacrifices as with Baal worship, to assure a good planting and bountiful harvest. Once a crop was planted, sacrifices to other gods were required to bring rain. The problem was that all these gods required human time and attention and often blood to satisfy the many different areas of one's daily living. One ran nearly ragged trying to keep up with them all.

The difference between them and the Old Testament Hebrews was their belief summarized in the great Shemah: "Hear, O Israel: The Lord our God, the Lord is one" (Deut 6:4). What a radical claim that was, for it asserts the complete authority of one God, and one alone. Upon this command rests all the further revealed qualities of God: he loves his people; he will protect and provide for them; he will bless them. At the same time, however, certain repercussions are clearly stipulated for those who fail to serve God, for many of "God's people" failed to serve him. In fact, many ran right back to all the pagan idols to try to make it their own way.

The early centuries of the Christian church were slow to let go of the primitive theology of multiple powers. It was a church under persecution. Surely the question arose: Why, if we are believers in God, and his Son who overcame death and evil, can pain continue to pursue us? All kinds of answers surfaced in the early centuries of the church. God is all powerful, but doesn't care about us. God is not really all powerful, for there must be a force equal to, or more powerful than, him. Perhaps Jesus's crucifixion, then, was not the deed of a Savior, but of a deluded prophet.

During the tumultuous early period of fourth-century history, Saint Augustine did much to set the benchmark of our modern understanding of good and evil. For some time he had been an adherent of the popular Manichean heresy, originated by an obscure Babylonian. Basically, Mani argued that good and evil are two co-eternal forces existing in a dualistic tension. Evil may be rendered harmless and ineffectual if humans learn to live by certain rules and live according to the "God-sent mind." Then, when one dies, one will be redeemed from imprisonment in the body and released to a true home. The idea may seem rather bizarre to orthodox Christians today. Yet, the concept of God and Satan in some sort of heavyweight duel for the cosmos does prevail in many religions.

The perversity of the Manichean heresy, as Augustine discovered, is two-fold. First, it made the ultimate rule of good contingent upon human decisions. Second, our personal salvation is a matter of our own actions. Consequently, Augustine concluded that "I sought 'whence is evil,' and sought in an evil way; and saw not the evil in my very search."[1]

In the argument that follows, Augustine raises literally dozens of questions but can't quite shrug the action of evil from the shoulders of the individual will. And if that is so, even if Satan continues to lure us to evil and even though God is forever our great deliverer, even unto eternal life, then evil arises from some essential malignancy in the human soul. It is a case of our incapacity to will the things that we should and would do, and giving in to what we should not do. Or, as St. Paul said, "What I want to do I do not do, but what I hate I do" (Rom 7:15). The difference with Paul is that he desires to serve Christ fully in gratitude for his salvation.

A host of implications arises from Augustine's argument in his *Confessions*, some of which he deals with at length, others only passingly. Indeed, we might even ask what relevance do his arguments bear to us today? To answer this we have to work as much by implications as by actual arguments. We have to read the words between the words. Augustine refuses to situate good and evil as two opposed and eternal powers. God is the sole eternal power. Augustine freely admits that his reading of the Apostle Paul initiated this step of his conversion from Manicheanism. Although not clearly articulated in his writings, it would seem to follow that Augustine accepted Paul's beliefs about origins and God's creation. For example, Paul made it clear that everything God made is good (1 Tim 4:4). He made it clear also that "every good and perfect gift" is from God (Jas 1:17). On the other hand, Paul points out the dilemma that "There is no one who does good" (Rom 3:12).

Augustine then concludes that God, the Good, is almighty. Consequently, evil is always a lesser manifestation of good, a "deprivation" of good just as illness or death is a deprivation of life. So evil is never an independent body. It is a parasite. There is no pure evil for then it would be

---

1. Augustine, *Confessions*, 123.

nothing. Yet, humans choose evil simply because they don't focus on God, the absolute good, but instead want to satisfy their own proud desires.

Augustine's views sharpened dramatically when, after fourteen years of labor and in his seventy-second year, he issued his theological and philosophical masterpiece, *City of God*. *The Confessions* is his spiritual autobiography, one sinner coming to Christ. However moving the narrative, the arguments often consist of undeveloped insights and rather spontaneous commentary. In *City of God* his arguments are much more refined, strategically developed, and elegant. Yet the major imprint that Augustine left over later centuries is his insistence on the following: 1) that in no way are good and evil equal and eternal powers; 2) that God is almighty and all good; 3) that evil has something to do with the waywardness of the human will. There is hardly enough in Augustine to please all Christian doctrines sixteen-hundred years later. And sixteen-hundred years later denominations do indeed vary on many of the fine points of understanding the presence of evil in this world. Nonetheless, there is some common ground in these fundamentals.

Doctrine is one way to understand the presence of pain, but there is another.

So often, theology sharpens on the whetstone of great calamity. We always have our personal pain to deal with, those times when we mouth our pleas for deliverance before God. There are times, however, when we stand back aghast and are struck dumb with the thought—how on earth could this happen? Sometimes we can even capture those events by dates: 9/11/2001, D-Day, and such. Then we sort through the imponderable sneer of evil once more, stunned by the pain inflicted.

A key date in the fourteenth century set the Western world adrift. Augustine's emphasis upon philosophy to put evil in its place, to diminish the active agency of Satan, and to confine evil to wayward human choices twisted askew like wet newspapers in a windstorm. In fact, many referred to it as "the Face of Satan."

It was spawned in Asia and arrived at the seaports of Italy by spring, 1345. It was powerful and malevolent, wreaking its disaster trail like a hurricane. Nor was there any shelter for the people from the storm—no cures, no escape. In fact, by the time it retracted from Europe in 1348, nearly half of Europe's population had died. It made its last stand in England in 1348, devastating the population in the same way. It even had a name: The Black

Death, named after tumors that grew to the size of softballs and turned deep purple/black before exploding open.

So virulent and disfiguring was the disease that people refused to go near corpses, leaving them to rot where they had fallen. People wouldn't touch them, nor their clothing or possessions. Bodies stacked up in the streets, nurturing rats who spread the disease further. Some people earned a little money carrying the corpses to the church cemetery where they were piled into trenches.

And what about those churches? What about the priests, the intercessors with God? The people believed this was a punishment by God. They longed for some answers from their spiritual authorities. For the most part, any church officials who could afford it, or could rob enough from the church till, sequestered themselves from the people in fortified strongholds. The human tie between the people and God disappeared in the night.

Just as bad as the failure of intercessory tasks was another very fundamental reality. The only medical resources available to these people were quack remedies and ineffectual herbal traditions. For example, at the first indication of plague, one was to wash the body down with a mixture of vinegar and potato mash. Tumors were most often dug open with a dull knife. The medicine of priestly prayers may have been more effective. But 40 percent of the clergy who hadn't fled died of the plague. Gradually, as the death rate spiraled past one out of every three people, they were denied the one spiritual comfort they had left—Last Rites. The people staggered under the wrath of God with no one to set the story straight.

Plague receded like the ashes after a devastating fire. But it did not end. In fact, recurrences ran their course throughout the rest of the fourteenth century and not until the seventeenth century could one say that Europe was free of the plague. After the ashes, however, people were left to contemplate this wildfire of pain that had ripped through their lives.

Their first thoughts had been that God was passing some horrible judgment upon them. Like some ancient petitioners to a stone god, groups of people called flagellants staggered from town to town whipping themselves as a walking sacrifice. All the traditional means of reaching out to God and of receiving his presence were overturned. The great silence filled with the great pain and no one knew quite what to say.

In a very real sense these two events—the careful theological thinking of Augustine and the chaotic experience of plague—shape the bookends of human understanding of evil. How do we understand the presence of pain in our lives? Do we bring to this basic question careful philosophical system? Do we speak out of personal experience, searching for our own answers?

When attempting to define the source of evil and the cause of pain, we might do well to follow Georgia's pattern: the seed, the root, and the condition. Yet, I want to be very careful here to respect each individual's unique experiences. Therefore, I suggest some general answers instead of categorical ones, which I just don't think are very helpful. We are humans, individual children of God, and we can't all be jammed into similar categories.

That leaves us two sources for pain, both of which we have touched upon in the historical overview. First, pain, if impossible to locate in a good, loving, and omnipotent source, must then stem from an evil, malign, and limited source. We name it as Devil, its father as Satan. The second source must be something within humanity itself that is the cause of pain. Since many very good people suffer unspeakable pain, we cannot say that this cause is particular or individual. Rather, we say it is something common to human nature itself. We are "born into" it, if you will. This second option we call "the fall," tracing it to Eden where Adam and Eve first turned from God's will to their own will.

Let's consider each of these in turn, examining the biblical evidence for both as sources of pain.

The Father of Lies

The first thing we must understand about Satan is that he has great power, but he never has as much power as God. I'm not particularly fussy about the physical details of Satan, whether he "prowls around like a roaring lion looking for someone to devour" as Peter pictured him (1 Pet 5:8), or whether he is depicted as some monster from the infernal regions who sends his demons out on attack, or as the suave and cunning seducer as C. S. Lewis pictured him in *The Screwtape Letters*. If anything, we moderns have devalued Satan. We either depict him as a cartoon buffoon (horns and tail) or we just don't talk about him. For that matter, we don't talk much about evil either.

The belief in the existence of Satan has so diminished in our time that he seems to have passed into some ancient mythology. He is part of a story that is outmoded, that cannot fit into any rational context, and that answers to no technological investigation. All of this, no doubt, is precisely how Satan prefers it. It makes his work so very much easier when others are not aware of his work. Perhaps one of the most dangerous things believers can do with Satan is to belittle his presence or power.

This is all really quite odd, since earlier eras had a much keener sense of Satan's reality. Indeed, so does scripture. In the Old Testament he is depicted as the Adversary, and one who works evil among God's chosen people (see especially the story of Job). In the New Testament, when Jesus's redemptive mission is underway, the activity of this Adversary becomes far more concerted, both against Jesus's ministry and also that of the new church. He is called "prince of this world" (John 14:30) and "prince of the power of the air" (Eph 2:2). He is always shown as hostile to God and working to thwart the purposes of God. Numerous passages of Satan's malignancy occur. The sum of them is this: Satan and God's mission—to redeem the world through the sacrifice of Jesus and the work of the church—are in a mighty conflict. They were in the first century; they are today.

The sense of this conflict led many early believers into an odd heresy. Yes, they agreed, Satan and God, evil and good, are in supreme conflict. How will the conflict end? Well, it depends on human actions. If the majority of us make the right choices the majority of the time, then God's kingdom will win. This, of course, was Augustine's challenge. This heresy emphasizes humans working out their own salvation, rather than through Jesus.

But there are other rational roadblocks to this thinking of Satan and God being equal powers, one for evil and one for good. For one thing, as the church fathers taught, evil is derivative and parasitical. We can't know evil purely, nor can we know evil apart from good. In his important book *Not the Way It's Supposed to Be: A Breviary of Sin*, Cornelius Plantinga, Jr. describes the problem as perversion:

> Perversion is an ends-and-purposes disease. Most broadly understood, perversion is the turning of loyalty, energy, and desire away from God and God's project in the world: it is the diversion of construction materials for the city of God to side projects of our own, often accompanied by jerry-built ideologies that seek to justify the diversion.[2]

The evidence suggests that theologically and philosophically Satan is always secondary to God and in no way shares equal status.

We ask ourselves why it is necessarily so that Satan is always secondary to God. First, we believe that God is Creator; therefore, Satan must be creature—a being created by God. Given his essential nature of being good,

2. Plantinga, *Not the Way It's Supposed to Be*, 40.

just, and righteous, God cannot create an evil being, else he would no longer be good or just or righteous. (One of the better discussions I have seen of this issue appears in the second half of C. S. Lewis' "The Pain of Animals" in *God in the Dock*.)

Satan, therefore, must have been created good. But of his own volition, he chose against good. Scripture gives us three proofs for this claim. First, in his prophetic vision, Isaiah describes what many commentators see as the fall of Satan from heaven:

> How you have fallen from heaven,
> O morning star, son of the dawn!
> You have been cast down to the earth,
> You who once laid low the nations!
> You said in your heart,
> "I will ascend to heaven;
> I will raise my throne
> above the stars of God;
> I will sit enthroned on the mount of assembly,
> on the utmost heights of the sacred mount.
> I will ascend above the tops of the clouds;
> I will make myself like the Most High."
> But you are brought down to the grave,
> to the depths of the pit.
> (Isa 14:12–15)

Not only does Isaiah see the fall, he also gives the reason: Satan wanted to be like God. It was an act of pride, the same temptation he offered to Adam and Eve.

The second proof comes from the life of Jesus. Jesus had just sent out the seventy-two disciples to prepare the "harvest." In time they returned, exclaiming, "Lord, even the demons submit to us in your name" (Luke 10:17). Jesus responds: "I saw Satan fall like lightning from heaven" (Luke 10:18). Astonishing words. They confirm that (1) Satan did get cast out of heaven as Isaiah said, and (2) Jesus was there as the eternal Son of God.

The third proof comes from an angel of God, this time speaking to John in his Revelation. Early in the book John repeatedly emphasizes that Satan's work is alive and powerful (Rev 2:9, 2:13, 3:9). In the vision, however, John reveals the final end of Satan, also referred to as the beast or the dragon. Satan's reign will end; he, and all his demons, will be cast forever into the lake of burning sulfur to be "tormented day and night for ever and ever" (Rev 21:10). In his always illuminating study *God, Pain, and Evil*,

George Buttrick argues that "The devil's power involves suffering, but it is a transient power"[3] God, who possesses the authority of dominion, sets the terminal point for the devil's power.

Such authority reminds me of God's majestic recitation beginning in Job 38:

> Who shut up the sea behind doors
> when it burst forth from the womb,
> When I made the clouds its garment
> and wrapped it in thick darkness,
> When I fixed limits for it
> and set its doors and bars in place,
> When I said, "This far you may come
> and no farther;
> here is where your proud waves halt"?
> (8–11)

The creator God imposes order on his creation by establishing limits. Satan is one such creation; it is inconceivable that his wrong can extend past God's just limits.

Where does that leave us? Let's summarize. Satan was once an angel of light, created by God. In his pride he wanted to be like God, and thus was cast out of heaven. God cannot abide evil in his presence. In our present lives, Satan does bear the power to afflict God's people as he attempts to thwart the work of the kingdom of God. In the last day, Satan will be bound in the lake of fire, unable to inflict his malignancy upon God's people anymore. Jesus has won the victory over evil. Satan does not have the final word. However powerful Satan may seem—and he is—he is a Satan in handcuffs, awaiting the last judgment.

Human Nature

We commonly, almost passingly, trace the seed of human pain to Adam and Eve submitting to the temptation in the Garden of Eden. This common doctrine, however, should be received with caution—in capital letters. It opens the creaky door to that old excuse: "It's my fallen nature. I really couldn't help myself." In fact, you could and should help yourself. One can only imagine Paul's exasperation when he writes to the Romans: "What

---

3. Buttrick, *God, Pain, and Evil,* 66.

shall we say, then? Shall we go on sinning so that grace may increase? By no means!" (Rom 6:1–2). Paul took sin seriously, as well we should.

Sin is a serious matter. We need to think of sin in human nature in two ways. First, the essential meaning of sin, in the words of George Buttrick, "is the denial of God and the pride and presumption by which we attempt to play our own God."[4] In this sense, sin is any act that contravenes God's authority, express commandment, or general revelation. Always, in such acts, humans put their desires first and "play God." Second, in addition to understanding sin as an act, sin is a presumption of mind and a betrayal of trust. Sin is an act "against." Against whom, though? Against any human, animal, or other component of the created order, surely, but especially against God who is our only deliverance from sin. Therefore also, sin is a betrayal of trust, not just in the violation of God's commandment but also because we have willingly separated ourselves from the hope of deliverance in the act of sinning. Sin, then, is both an action and a state of mind.

In *The City of God*, Saint Augustine uses a very nice analogy, explaining the effect of sin upon a person like the effect of blindness on the eye.

> Sin is to a nature what blindness is to an eye. The blindness is an evil or defect which is a witness to the fact that the eye was created to see the light and, hence, the very lack of sight is the proof that the eye was meant, more than any other member of the body, to be the one particularly capable of seeing the light. Were it not for this capacity, there would be no reason to think of blindness as a misfortune . . . The very sin which deprived this nature of happiness in God and left it miserable is the best proof of how good that nature was, as it came from the hand of God.[5]

The effect of sin, although undertaken for momentary pleasure perhaps, is always to diminish us in the long run. It's like taking a wedding dress, and dragging it repeatedly through the mud. Or, worse yet, doing so to the bride. Sin sullies the image of God in us.

To understand that temptation scene in Eden more clearly, to understand how it shapes our understanding of sin, and to understand how it becomes the seed of pain, let's revisit the event that changed history and reshaped human nature for all time.

The essential thing to remember about God's creation is that he created it "good." Three crucial phrases accompany the Genesis account of

4. Ibid., 74.
5. Augustine, *City of God*, 252.

creation. "And it was so" describes the immediacy of God's creation. He had no need of intermediary devices or agents. No special hocus-pocus appeared. He spoke the word and it happened. God is the only all-sufficient authority.

The second phrase, "And there was," is an announcement of achievement. God's word has been perfectly fulfilled. His word now stands in concrete form.

The third phrase, and the critical one here, is "it was good." We might give the phrase short shrift, saying something like, "If it came from God, of course it had to be good." Truth lies in that, but the dimensions of it are far larger.

What do we mean by the term "good" when we associate it with God? We know biblically that the goodness of God lies in such intrinsic qualities as lovingkindness, harmony (that is, God can't contradict himself), order, justice, and the like. If, then, God called his creation "good," it carries those very same qualities by which we know God to be good. Creation itself was orderly; it was harmonious (all parts fitting together as a seamless whole); it was just, with no intrinsic injustice in it; and it evidenced the nature of God's lovingkindness at every turn. It was good.

How did the good creation change to what Paul described thus: "We know that the whole earth has been groaning as in the pains of childbirth right up to the present time" (Rom 8:22)? How did our world of lovingkindness—as part of its very nature—become a world haunted by the grim face of pain lurking at the windows of our lives? To answer that, we have to turn to the "fall" of humanity and all the earth.

Before we do, note this caution. As one old song has it, "This Is My Father's World" (1901). The author, Maltbie D. Babcock, loved to hike in the hills of New York, viewing farms and pastureland below. Sometimes Babcock commented, "I'm going out to view my Father's world," from which the words of the song arose. Look particularly at the words of the third stanza:

> This is my Father's world.
> O let me ne'er forget
> That though the wrong seems oft so strong,
> God is the ruler yet.
> This is my Father's world:
> Why should my heart be sad?
> The Lord is King; let the heavens ring!
> God reigns; let the earth be glad!

God has not given up control of this world to the disharmonious—the perversion of justice and harmony—or to distortion of goodness.

Nonetheless, these things happen. No pain surfaced in Eden until humanity invited it in. No malevolence lay in the shadows until the Tempter slithered in with his sugared lies. No guilt or shame afflicted Adam and Eve as they tended the garden until they abused it for their own desires.

The key words there as we understand pain and suffering in a fallen world are "desires." Here we tie together the beguiling nature of Satan and human nature. We just examined the fact that Satan was expelled from heaven because he wanted to be like God. This arrogant creature wasn't just suspended; it was expelled. It will never see heaven again. That fundamental sin, however, lives on in fallen humanity. If we desire something, we too often impulsively grab it for no other reason than that we desire it.

In her book *Total Truth*, Nancy Pearcey examines the premise that "evil and disorder are not intrinsic in the material world but are caused by human sin, which takes God's good creation and distorts it to evil purposes."[6] In a sense, Pearcey's argument is correct. Material things cannot choose to do wrong. They cannot exercise will to follow their desires rather than God's desires of harmonious, just, and loving. But beyond question our material earth, and perhaps our material universe, has been fractured by disharmony since the Fall. Yes, there can be enormous goodness evidenced in the material world. No, it is not good in and of itself. As such, a certain kinship exists between human and material worlds.

Too often, perhaps, we cast dark and disparaging eyes on the sins of others. It is easy to do so; that sin is not mine, after all. And so we also lie to ourselves, because even the best of us share a fundamental nature with the overt sinner whom we are quick to judge. That common nature arises particularly in this matter of desire. We all wish for things; we turn, sometimes errantly, to possess them by any means. Why? Because they give us pleasure, they satisfy us, they provide us fun. And it is in the measurement of that desire for fun that, like Eve, distinctions blur and a sense of God's direction and awareness dim like a thick haze settling around us. In his revolutionary book, *Whatever Became of Sin?*, Karl Menninger is quite explicit:

> There is some "fun" in most sinning. Perhaps in a way we assume this to be the motive for it. The anticipated pleasure makes for the

6. Pearcey, *Total Truth*, 84.

greater temptation of it. Not all acts of sin have the same meaning
or degree of pleasure-giving function.[7]

Menninger adds that the satisfactions that accrue from sin for the individual outweigh cultural conformity or moral authority.

Perhaps this discussion can be tied together by one salient example.
What are those things to which we turn to have fun—at least as we view fun
through human desire? The Bible provides two very clear examples. Turn
to Deuteronomy 5 and see how many of these traditional warnings stand
in the way of human desire. Then turn to Matthew 5 and read Jesus's pro-
nouncements on many of those same warnings or laws. Then ask yourself,
how many of these, very specifically, are the reasons humans that you know
choose to sin.

The point I am working toward here is this. Pain can beset fallen humanity in two ways. First, we live in a natural order that in its post-fall state
is often injurious and harmful. It can cause pain. Shark bites hurt. So do
tetanus shots, sprained ankles, and headaches. Moreover, it doesn't seem
harmonious that they should cause pain. The list is extensive, including
diseases that ruin our bodies, stresses that wrack our brains, and events that
skew our lives. Something is out of order.

Second, pain can beset fallen humanity by individual or corporate
choices we make. Strip-mining coal from the mountains of West Virginia
and southeast Ohio must have seemed like a very good idea to many people
once. But now the ruined landscapes, the poisoned streams laden with sulfur, and the toxic mine tailings will haunt generations hence. Similarly, a
spouse's "one night—or hour—stand" will inflict damage to her and everyone who loves her.

What conclusions do we draw, then, at this point? Satan's nature has
not changed. Not in Eden, not now. He still wants to thwart God's good
work in any conceivable way and we are all too easy subjects for him to
work on. We certainly don't follow the example of Joseph when tempted
by Potiphar's wife—turn and run. We turn from sin with all the haste of
a tranquilized sloth. Satan continues to lure us through desire and pride.

The three stages of temptation in Eden that introduced pain into this
world are eerily similar to all our temptations. First, Satan raises doubt
about what God really meant: "Did God really say, 'You must not eat from
any tree in the garden'?" (Gen 3:1). In response, Eve echoes God's precise
command. We notice, furthermore, that Eve is separated from her mate at

7. Menninger, *Whatever Became of Sin?*, 183–84.

this critical juncture. The worst temptations come when we are alone. No wonder Genesis calls the serpent "wily" or "crafty."

The second stage of the temptation is to contradict God and appeal to pride. Satan denies God: "You will not surely die" (3:4). But now he twists Eve's knowledge of God all askew: "God knows that when you eat of it your eyes will be opened, and you will be like God, knowing good and evil" (3:5). In the first stage Satan lies. Now he subtly twists the truth to his ends. Yes, God knows good and evil. Yes, if Eve succumbs to the temptation, she too, and Adam following, will know good and evil. But the clincher here is the line that you will be like God. It is the same act of pride for which Satan was cast out of heaven.

The third stage, as we move from raising doubt to the outright lie, is emotional desire. That was the final act for Eve. Notice how she views it: "When the woman saw that the fruit of the tree was good for food and pleasing to the eye, and also desirable for gaining wisdom, she took some and ate of it" (3:6). You can place nearly any temptation you can think of into those three stages Eve went through and it will lead to the same end. It looks good, it's beautiful, we desire it = temptation, a step away from God, and the consequent pain.

So why pain? That is precisely what God sentences Adam and Eve to when he confronts them. Eve will suffer "pain in childbearing"; Adam in "painful toil" as he works the ground. With Adam and Eve, we too partake in the sentence. But why?

In Eden God and humanity lived in perfect trust. Adam and Eve, in order to keep that trust whole, had only to obey God's one command not to eat of the fruit of the tree of knowledge of good and evil. God didn't want them to have his knowledge. Only God knew how devastating such knowledge could be. This was the first covenant, a fidelity built on trust. A covenant is successful, however, only when both parties freely assent to it and follow it. Freely is the issue, for to validate the covenant humans also had the freedom to violate it. And they did.

The rupture that followed the breaking of the covenant of trust is hard to describe in human terms. One old analogy depicts God as an artist having created a beautiful canvas of creation, and then someone throws black paint on it. The analogy hardly does the reality justice. This was a rupture that worked through all humanity, through all the earth, and for all we know through all the cosmos. We went from trust to alienation, from ease in the garden to pain in the wilderness, and from talking intimately with God to mortal loneliness.

In *Not the Way It's Supposed to Be*, Cornelius Plantinga, Jr. describes this as a "vandalism of shalom." Plantinga ties this "vandalism" to the first sin in Eden and the consequent pain humanity suffers. He writes: "Sin is disruption of created harmony and then resistance to divine restoration of that harmony. Above all, sin disrupts and resists the vital human relationship to God."[8] This disruption of shalom—the harmonious accord—is the seed of pain in Eden's garden.

What exactly grew from this seed? What suffering assaults us? First, physical pain. Eve's pain in childbearing passes to all generations. Pain is our heritage. Second, Adam's pain is human labor, the frustration and sweat of work that had formerly been a delight. Third, the earth itself suffers pain, now producing "thorns and thistles" instead of abundant fruit. Fourth, the pain of death arises from the seed: "From dust you are and to dust you will return" (Gen 3:19). And, finally, the pain of alienation from God arises from the seed. From walking with God in the garden, Adam and Eve are banished from God's presence to wander in the wilderness.

It is easy to find roots for pain, as Georgia said that steamy night in the recovery house. We are in pain because a loved one died. That's the root of our sorrow and suffering. But where does that root come from? To answer that we have to find the seed. Only then can we begin to understand and come to grips with our experience with pain.

I still hear Georgia's deep voice echoing in my ears, in my mind. "The real seed," she had said, "is that I needed someone to lift the load. I needed Jesus."

Because even in Eden, in the wreckage of our seed of destruction, God planted a promise. Even before God announced the necessary consequence (the term most often used here, curse, is not quite accurate) of humanity's discord, he provided an answer. The serpent was indeed cursed, condemned to slither along the ground. But God promises that a distant offspring of Adam and Eve would crush the serpent's head (3:15), even while the serpent strikes the heel of that chosen one. The serpent may strike, but the chosen one will crush.

"The real seed is that I needed someone to lift the load. I needed Jesus."

---

8. Plantinga, *Not the Way It's Supposed to Be*, 5.

Chapter Three

I Hurt All Over

Physical Pain

She seemed very small then, at age four. Small and vulnerable.

When we are young parents we enjoy the lovely gifts of our children, never dreaming that things might go wrong, never guessing what grown up sorrow might come their way and trample their lives. In one of my favorite poems, "Spring and Fall," the Jesuit priest Gerard Manley Hopkins depicts a little girl named Margaret in a grove of trees. It is autumn, and all about her golden leaves are falling from the trees. And Margaret, the little girl, is crying. While she weeps for the fall of the leaves now, Hopkins writes, as she grows older she too will realize that it is the nature of all humanity to wither and die:

> It is the blight man was born for,
> It is Margaret you mourn for.

Even Hopkins's little girl will someday take her place in that train of physical pain.

My daughter, Tamara, did not cry. But she asked, "Why, Daddy?" And I felt my heart breaking. Fathers shouldn't have to explain hard things to four-year-old daughters. They have not the vocabulary, for all their learning.

At four, Tammy had developed a profound vocabulary all of her own. In that delightful art of learning language she pronounced with emphasis and pride her own variations. She wanted to go to the restaurant for a "hangleburg," and wear her hair in "cowtails." With some anatomical imagination, she declared that girls and moms have "blomblooms" and daddies have "peepers." She loved her pet, Lasha, her "little, shaggy, waggly-tailed dog."

These are the words that delight any parent. They reside in memory like a light sweetness.

But not these. At her two-year physical, the pediatrician observed, rather nonchalantly at the time, "Tammy has what we call a 'funnel chest.' We'll have to watch that." At subsequent checkups it grew progressively worse. By age four surgery was required.

We conferred with the specialist with his X-ray charts. "These five ribs on each side of the sternum," he said, "curve inward. They're longer than normal. They push the sternum inward, like so, on the heart and lungs. We want to catch them early so the cardiopulmonary system can develop normally."

"How?" we asked.

"It's not a particularly dangerous procedure. We clip the ends of the ribs pressing the sternum inward back to normal size. Then we wire a metal brace into the sternum to lift it up. Although," he added, "the recovery is quite painful."

My imagination went wild. Cut ribs, wired plates. This was in the days before arthroscopic surgery. They would cut a lateral incision across her tiny chest and fold the skin back. "Will it leave a scar?" I asked.

"We do plastic surgery on the closure," he said, "She'll be able to wear a bikini and no one will see it."

Forgive me. That is when the heart of this father began to cry. Truly, I saw her no longer as my little "cow-tailed" daughter but as a grown woman going her own way.

The day of the surgery came. It would be fairly long—three to four hours. Save for Pat and me, the waiting room was quiet, virtually empty. Our pastor came to visit us. Suddenly four people burst in, hysterical with fear. Crying loudly in great rasps. Collapsing into chairs. Then more, by twos and fours. The noise was deafening. Their daughter—sister, niece, a police officer—had been caught in a shoot-out and was critically wounded. She was undergoing emergency surgery for three gunshot wounds.

The waiting room seemed to tilt and grow dizzy. Our pastor had other calls to make, a schedule to keep. Many people were in pain. We knelt there on the far side of the waiting room, joining hands—Pat, our pastor, and I—and quietly began to pray for Tammy's surgery.

And the room fell silent. The police officer's relatives closed their eyes and fell silent, and many fell to their knees. Our pastor's voice rose slightly as he included that family in his prayer, as he prayed for that daughter. For in that moment of prayer, she seemed to be ours also. In that moment of prayer, she was God's daughter.

We need to understand two primary points in this chapter. First, physical pain varies in degree from person to person. There is no "one pain fits all." Second, physical pain affects the whole person, not just the site of the wound. I use the term "wound" in this chapter for the apparent source of pain. Clearly, however, pain affects one beyond that specific place. Physical pain inevitably has emotional, spiritual, and other effects as well.

The Language of Physical Pain

Physical pain is the kind we think of most frequently when that word is spoken. Indeed, some people, we sometimes believe, speak about their physical pain altogether too much, and often in too graphic detail. We try to change the subject. Nonetheless, we are all well acquainted with this pain, we can most readily pinpoint the source, we can readily find others who commiserate with our pain. Physical pain rides in the saddle of universal suffering. When we grieve for ourselves, we grieve for all humankind.

For that very reason—because physical pain is so often talked about—the words might well have lost their force. Perhaps you have had it when, just after your recovery from an illness, someone asks you how you're doing, then proceeds to deliver a lengthy discourse on his or her personal experience with the illness. Or, in a high stakes game of one-upmanship, someone will tell you about someone else who died of the illness. You almost want to say something like, "Aw, shucks! They got to the Promised Land before I did. I guess the Lord has some work for me to do yet and I better get busy with it."

If only we could say everything that readily comes to mind. But then there's that small matter of James's view: "The tongue also is a fire, a world of evil among the parts of the body. It corrupts the whole person, sets the whole course of his life on fire, and is itself set on fire by hell" (3:6). But in its own way, physical pain skewers our ability to find adequate descriptive words. Something shuts down in our brains as pain swarms in. We can't possibly sit back and rationally study the proposition of a broken elbow. We hurt and need help.

Because of that very inadequacy of a language for pain (can it only be measured by blips on some hospital machine?), people writing about pain use descriptive portraits or metaphors. Emily Dickinson, who wrote mostly about the interior pain of her depressive disorder, wrote:

> Pain—has an Element of Blank—
> It cannot recollect
> When it begun—or if there were
> A time when it was not—

For Dickinson, the present experience of pain is so overwhelming that one cannot remember a life lived without it.

Doctors may ask you to assign a numerical value to your pain—on a scale of one (minor) to ten (major), how would you describe your pain? We assign numbers when words fail us. Pain may be describable, as in metaphors for example, but it is always inexpressible in precise terms. "You have a ruptured appendix" describes something wrong with the body and nothing about the degree of pain. Just where and how, then, might the "inexpressible" receive voice? When bodily pain reduces us to a groan, prayer gives us the vocabulary of the Holy Spirit interceding for us. "The Spirit" Paul declares, "helps us in our weakness. We do not know what we ought to pray for, but the Spirit himself intercedes for us with groans that words cannot express" (Rom 8:26). The very inexpressibility of language when one languishes in pain, those spoken or unspoken groans, are received by the Holy Spirit and offered to God in a divine understanding. Even when you can only groan, when your pain has an element of blank that turns you inward, God listens, his ear pressed very close to capture every sound.

Individual Pain

In confronting pain, each person's experience is intimately individual. When my mother was dying of cancer, she was miffed that for the first time in her adult life she had to wear pants instead of her self-sewn dresses to radiation treatments. If I know my mother, I think she was glad when the radiation was pronounced useless and she wouldn't have to suffer the indignity of pants again. Men wore pants, not ladies—and my mother was every inch a lady.

In another situation, a colleague of mine elected to have his chemo done during the night so that he could get all his vomiting done before teaching his first class.

Yet another colleague gave a chapel talk as his final appearance at the college. He sat in a chair, too weak to stand, and spoke to the crowded listeners. As he closed, he took off his watch and held it up. "I no longer hear the ticking of time," he said, "but the first seconds of eternity." He began to sing softly, as the audience joined in, "My Jesus, I Love Thee." The song crescenoed on final verse:

> In mansions of glory and endless delight,
> I'll ever adore thee in heaven so bright;
> I'll sing with the glittering crown on my brow:
> If ever I loved thee, my Jesus, 'tis now.

The speaker was silent during that last verse. Instead, he held the watch to his ear, looked upward, and smiled.

The audience filed out. It seemed that leftover notes still rang everywhere in the chapel, so full of song it had been.

We hate physical suffering in part because it is so evident. We need care, sometimes the highly specialized care of hospitals, surgeries, clinics, rehab centers. And we hate it because it changes something substantial about ourselves—our bodies. We have to learn to make do in new ways; too often we have to give up the old. It may be the young soccer player who seriously fractures her leg. It may be the former hotshot tennis and racquetball player who now can hardly walk because of osteoarthritis in his knees. It may be the elderly shut-in whose great comfort has been to read and now suffers from macular degeneration. The world moves from shades of gray to darkness.

Physical pain marks our susceptibility as human creatures. We stand in need, and, for some of us, very vulnerable for the first time in our lives. Never before has medical science understood so much about the process or mechanism of pain.

The June 4, 2007, issue of Newsweek ran a cover story on "The New War on Pain." Observing that "chronic pain is one of the most pervasive and intractable medical conditions in the United States," the issue explored recent scientific methods to identify and treat the source of pain. With one in five Americans suffering from chronic pain, the annual medical cost for treating pain runs to approximately $61 billion in lost productivity and medical fees.[1]

---

1. Carmichael, "The War on Pain," 41–42.

This article focused solely upon physical injury and pain. For example, it defined the scientific route that an ankle injury takes to the brain, and how the brain perceives the nature of pain and its source. This topography of pain has been ably charted in many sources. Pull down MayoClinic.com on the Internet, for example, and under NERVOUS SYSTEM, a site called "How you feel pain" gives you a tidal wave of scientific/medical information. Moreover, it has related links to other sites such as "phantom pain."

In daily activity, as Paul Brand, MD, and Philip Yancey have pointed out in their book *The Gift of Pain*, this work of the neurosystem is a good and essential thing in our daily health. The authors take as their example Dr. Brand's work with Hansen's disease (leprosy). The greatest danger with the loss of this pain-signaling system due to leprosy is that the body doesn't signal the danger. For example, a leper can severely burn a foot, and not be fully aware of the damage until infection sets in. If the infection is too severe, the foot must be amputated.

Seen in this way, the pain-signaling device of the neurosystem is a good thing. Without it, we would have to live hermetically sealed lives to avoid even the possibility of injury. Physical pain is useful. It indicates our need and turns us toward avoidance or treatment.

But, as the *Newsweek* article points out, the experience of pain is variable. That is to say, your blister from a 5k run might hurt you a great deal more than mine does. Why? Perhaps your heels aren't as calloused as mine. Or, perhaps you made the mistake of wearing new running shoes and the blister went deeper than mine. Perhaps, as a veteran runner I'm simply more accustomed to the pain of an occasional blister. As *Newsweek* says, however, "One patient's 7 may be another's 4."[2] We simply cannot categorize the pain of others into a "one-size-fits-all."

The trouble with physical pain is that each person's brain processes it in so many different ways that sometimes successful treatment can't be found. We are all aware, for example, of the phenomenon of phantom pain. A person might fall and slam an elbow hard against the sidewalk. Immediately the tender ganglion of nerves screams pain to the brain. Often, perhaps with a pain-reliever, the feeling subsides. But long after that the brain still feels the trauma and signals pain from the elbow. Phantom pain is common in survivors of battlefield wounds, particularly those who endure amputation of a limb. For years these veterans perceive acute pain in the missing limb.

2. Ibid., 43.

In *Pain: The Fifth Vital Sign*, Marni Jackson undertakes a daunting research to find some means to reliably quantify pain. All other vital signs—blood pressure, temperature, pulse, respirations—are readily quantified. Why not pain, which seems more important than any of these? Even though Jackson's study might have most bearing upon those in medical fields, her personal experiences, such as having the anesthetic wear-off during dentistry, make it familiar to any of us. Pain comes as a rude and uninvited guest at the very worst possible time.

While modern neuroscience has carefully mapped out the sinuous course of pain from injury to the brain, too many variables intrude to make the route an easily understood one. Gender affects the experience of pain. Individual hormonal systems affect the experience of pain. Phenomena such as phantom pain affect the experience of pain. Our only safe conclusion is that we all experience pain, but we all experience it differently.

But this is also clear. All pain, whether short term or chronic, affects all aspects of life. I don't mean simply the physical limitations in what we can or cannot do because of pain. Rather, pain affects all aspects of who we are in life. It is not surprising that so many individual experiences of pain are also accompanied by depression.

While medical science marches onward in its understanding and treatment of pain, still untold, then, is the individual story. Necessarily so, for God has made us both fearfully and wonderfully (Ps 139:14).

Are There Any Directions?

In the midst of physical pain, from a hot blister on the heel to a body burning with fever, what can we do? Several steps are critical to our spiritual and physical well-being.

First, acknowledge your pain. By that I do not mean simply to consult your doctor, though of course you would want to do that. Rather, permit yourself the freedom to say, I hurt, I'm scared, I feel alone. Tell God those things. Permit yourself to talk with God in whatever way your emotions go. Drop that stiff upper lip. You have a perfect right to acknowledge your pain. You don't have to impress anyone, not even yourself, and especially not God.

The second stage is to ask for the support of others, particularly prayer support. You may remember that in chapter one we discussed ways in which people deny their pain. These ranged from a denial of the pain we ourselves suffer—that is, we'll get by on our own strength—to a fear that our pain might intrude upon the seemingly serene lives of others. Our hurt may be embarrassing. We don't want our intimate pain known. Despite these emotional impediments, we humans need the comfort and aid of others. Friends and family offer a first line of defense. Counselors and pastors offer another. Prayer support groups and prayer servants still another. While we need emotional support at our side, we also need others to do the hard work of prayer intercession. I have had points in my life when I just could not pray. The pain and stress were too great and my mind raced around immediate demands. That's when I needed others to stand in the gap for me.

That brings me to the third stage. I'm nervous about stating it: Trust God. I'm nervous because the phrase is sometimes used as a sop to people in pain—"Oh, just trust God." Sometimes it's even used negatively—"If only you had trusted God more, this wouldn't have happened." Yet, when our hearts are directionless in a maze of hurt, the one surety we have is to trust God for this fragile life we have. The well-known verse from Proverbs 3:5 has never diminished: "Trust in the Lord with all your heart and lean not on your own understanding." And David proclaims: "Some trust in chariots and some in horses, but we trust in the name of the Lord our God" (Ps 20:7). Such trust is not a matter of rational understanding alone. These texts don't have to be broken down and analyzed. The message is straightforward: Place all your pain, all your fear and anxiety, and all your suffering in God's hands.

Some of the early church mystics had a word for this: detachment. It means "letting go." When we can't handle it, we admit the fact and let it go into God's hands. Also, we let go of our pride, our inexorable will to chart our own way. We detach ourselves from that, and trust in God's way.

As Dr. Thomas Arnett tells the story, he had come home from a church meeting on October 14, 1987, and, feeling tired, went to bed. A short time later his wife heard unusual sounds from his side of the bed—the gasping for breath that precedes a full cardiac arrest. At the hospital where he himself worked as an OB/ GYN doctor, his heart was shocked into rhythm. His following reaction is shared by many who suffer pain:

> I was flown to Vanderbilt Hospital in Nashville, and the next two weeks revealed a lot about my character and my relationship with God. I remember being introspective, quiet, noncommunicative and most of all, angry at God. I didn't want to read my Bible or pray, and I spent endless hours watching the TV screen so I wouldn't have to think. After all, I had dedicated my life to God (or so I thought).[3]

3. Arnett, "The Valley of the Shadow of Death," 181.

In order to carry on, however, Arnett admits that he "stuffed" his emotions and "went on with my life."

Things changed, both physically and spiritually. Two more cardiac arrests and irregular heart rhythms assaulted him. It seemed that he had to go further down in his own strength before he could discover God's strength. Consequently, Dr. Arnett was able to distance himself from the intensity of his personal physical pain and discover spiritual lessons. In his situation, these were four:[4]

- God is in control whether I recognize it or not.
- I can choose my response to adversity, but I cannot choose whether I experience adversity or not.
- I do not know what the future holds (and here he quotes from Psalm 73:23–26).
- I have a faithful wife.

If, in the fourth position, we insert some prayer intercessor for us, then these are truths that can apply to any one of us.

And what of the police officer undergoing emergency surgery at the same moment Tammy's thoracic cavity was being restructured? It turned out that she had been shot six times, not three. But three of the wounds had struck her protective vest. After much rehabilitation, she returned to the force—although no longer on the streets.

And Tammy? The hardest part, we were told, would be three days after the surgery when they had to remove the epidural catheter. The tissue would have begun to heal around it. Nurses would have to hold her down while the doctor pulled the tube and closed the incision.

But when the time came, when two good-sized nurses braced her shoulders and knees against the anticipated reaction, she asked me to hold her shoulders.

I didn't want to. I didn't want to be associated with the expected pain. But I did. It was an issue of trust.

When the doctor rapidly pulled the tube, she barely flinched. She said, "Ouch," rather softly. The doctor and nurses looked at her in amazement.

"Can I go home now?" she said.

4. Ibid., 184.

Chapter Four

"It's All in Your Head"

The Pain of Mental Illness

THIS IS THE PAIN often spoken of in whispers, as if we were entering a funeral parlor. It is the pain that leaves people blinking, wondering if you are talking about something like a bad cold or like cancer. It is a pain that, as one person murmured to me once about an individual undergoing treatment for depression, "I think it's just something all in her head." I mulled the cruel irony. It was not in her head like an imaginary pain; yet it was very much all in her head.

Despite the breakneck pace of new learning on mental disorders during the last two decades, and despite the stunning success of medical treatments, pain of the mind is still one of the least understood disorders today. The reason is clear. Consider an example.

One of the popular sports in our part of Michigan is snowboarding on trails adjacent to ski runs. It's full of strange terms like "catching big air" and "in the pipe" and such. I understand, given my limited point of view of having done neither, that snowboarding is even more thrilling, dangerous, and exciting than skiing. Of course my youngest son Joel had to try it. How much different could it be from skateboarding? His sixth-grade class was in collusion with this dare-deviltry. It sponsored a weekend ski-club, with reduced rates even.

It wasn't too long before we got the call. Joel caught too much air. He went airborne. He needed a parachute coming down. Unfortunately, all he had was two arms, one of which snapped cleanly, both the ulna and radius. On top of his arm the two jagged edges protruded against the skin; about an inch below the other ends protruded against the bottom. I could almost feel the pain shooting along my own forearm.

A Biblical Understanding of Pain

We see the signs of physical pain. Although the pain of mental illness does evidence some physical and behavioral signs, the pain is largely hidden, tucked back in the synapses of the brain. The pain is nonetheless as real as Joel's broken arm, the effects as excruciating. Consider the case of one person whom I'll call Eric, and who has given permission to tell his story that way.

Eric has spent an adult lifetime fighting some kind of depression. He also denied depression more cleverly than anyone he had ever known. That has been part of the problem. Depression has been a sneaky adversary; they were nearly always sparring. Although Eric would like to look for outside causes for it—because then he could pretend to make them go away—he can't. The real cause is simply the maddening intricacies of this thing called a brain. A brain God endowed for Eric out of a lineage of several generations manifesting varying degrees of mental disorder. It pops up willy-nilly in the generational order, hopscotching over some and landing with a heavy thud on others.

For almost as long as Eric can remember, about three or so times a year, he endured a depressive episode that generally lasted about one to two weeks. During his forties, the bouts lasted longer—three weeks, say, instead of one. Those days were sometimes a battle for balance, walking a tightrope over a gray abyss, occasionally fingering moments of light, only to have them soon slip away. The problem was that the down periods were getting lower and lasting longer. Then a sequence of events, each of them difficult in and of themselves but now coiled together like a maelstrom, precipitated a decline he couldn't fight his way out of. Clearly, Eric needed help.

Help for mental health needs is not easy to get. First, one has to bang on the bronze gates of the insurance company; then one has to try to schedule an appointment sometime in the foreseeable future.

It was worth the work. A Christian doctor Eric finally saw—and still sees—is a man of eminent skill, insight, and compassion. The problem was that Eric had labored under a subterfuge of coping mechanisms for so long that he could identify little other than an inconsolable depression. Coping mechanisms? These are the ways a mentally ill person hides the illness from others and locks it tight inside. For Eric, the most successful of these was exercise. This occurred in part because Eric also understood, with a primitive, untutored understanding, the intrinsic restlessness of mind and body. What would later be diagnosed as ADHD (Attention Deficit/Hyperactive Disorder) was known to him only as a mental pinball machine, his mind careening with hopeless abandon from one little maze to another, purple and red lights flashing bizarrely. At its worst moments, thoughts rocketed through Eric's mind like meteors. At such times he could not sit in one place for more than a minute. He actually timed it occasionally, trying to understand and trying to stay the disintegration—like a man wondering how close he could walk to the edge of a cliff.

Like one hunted by a pack of baying hounds, Eric exercised to escape the slathering jaws. He would run for miles, letting the blessed endorphins jack through the brain. He would play racquetball and tennis with a pure ferocity mistaken by opponents for skill. Hard sports—where the sweat ran and the heart pounded and the lungs hurt. Pain as anodyne against pain.

It wasn't enough. One cannot, after all, run all day.

Therefore, the symptoms—moods and situations—seemed to be clear enough at the time. Classic for any clinical depression. A textbook case for ADHD also. Eric started on Prozac.

Eric was reborn on Prozac.

It was quick, thorough, and exhilarating.

Within a month he felt absolutely happy. How had he survived so long without this, his deliverance?

Prozac, where had you been all my life!

This is the way normal people live. Every day!

Euphoria.

And dangerous as a dream.

One is never weaker than when one feels like a god. Never more susceptible.

Like a blaze of glory Eric's euphoria kept elevating. Rocket boosters attached to the endorphins of his brain, billions of rushing gouts of flame off the tarmac pushing him higher and higher. Since it felt so good, he felt no need to inform his doctor of anything else. They had by now scheduled their meetings simply for "med checks" every few weeks, during which Eric would tell him that he felt great. No, he didn't feel any side effects from the Prozac. Not any! And, tellingly, Eric would add that he had never felt so good in his adult life.

Six months after starting Prozac, contrary feelings began to whiplash on a nearly daily basis. On some days Eric still seemed to be chugging upward on a rollercoaster whose top he couldn't see. The higher he got into those dizzying skies the more impaired his judgment became. Although he didn't know it at the time, this is one of the primary symptoms of bipolar disorder. Right and wrong become relative to one's mood and impulses.

All of our psychological fences have gates in them. We decide when to lock them, when to open them to step into the outside world, when to open them to let the outside world enter our own. Opening gates is dangerous; that's why one needs safe boundaries to begin with. We establish those by moral law, ethical reflection, religious traditions, and sound judgment. We learn—from our youth on—when to say yes or no.

But the bipolar heading toward the manic phase begins to see those boundary fences as mere obstacles, easily bypassed. Then perhaps they are only rocks to be stepped over, then mere pebbles in the road where the bipolar wants to go. Each lapse of judgment—of overstepping the boundaries—makes successive overstepping easier and seemingly more natural. It isn't hard, after all, to step over pebbles. One doesn't even know they're there. Many symptoms mark the bipolar life—the agonizing twists between elevation and depression that come as suddenly as storm, the unpredictability of mood and action, and the bewilderment about personhood. The lapses in judgment, however, are the most critical, each bearing dangerous effects to the person and his or her family.

Bipolars share an old line. Manics can fly, they say. It's the landing that kills you. Then, the pebbles so easily stepped over do indeed feel like a field of rocks.

By midsummer of that year, Eric was crashing backward, as if all the gears on the rollercoaster had simply sheared off. He would occasionally come down in the morning and say to his wife, "I think I'm losing a sense of myself." Or, "I just don't feel right anymore." Or, "I don't know who I am anymore." With that the depression would work like an insidious virus back into his brain. Worse, Eric could remember little or nothing (a well-documented effect) of events during the hypomania. He received a new diagnosis—mixed-state bipolar disorder with ADHD—which meant that he could cycle several times a day. It is impossible to retain a coherent memory pattern with a brain being whiplashed like a crooked centrifuge.

If the apex of a rollercoaster serves as an analogy for one side of the bipolar experience, there is that other, darker side to contend with. Indeed, it is all the darker for having danced in the sun. It is more than a precipitous plunge. It is the mind-cracking dislocation from light into blackness.

Down there, abandoned to the dark, one starts looking desperately for answers. One doesn't much care, after all, if one soars high as a kite psychologically. Darkness is another matter. For Eric it fueled the desire to pump enough information, enough clinical answers, like frantic CPR, into his bewildered brain so that he could say: It's okay. I understand. Clinical answers, however, never provide full understanding to account for the experience. That's because clinical answers are about people; depression is about the person. People who don't know much about it use the word *depression* as if you had a flat tire or a sinus infection. They don't know that it's an icicle that grows in the heart and reaches into the brain so that you want to lie under the covers and try to keep warm. Depression immobilizes you in every way possible and separates you from nearly any human nearby you.

On the basis of the evidence Eric provided his doctor, the initial diagnosis of depression certainly appeared correct. Also, the diagnosis of ADHD, that alphabet soup for a truant brain, had "sufficient and necessary evidence," as my training in philosophy has taught me to put it.

Furthermore, it is not at all unusual for depression to accompany ADHD, either from linked brain chemistry or from the confusion and shame frequently engendered from the inability to perform in classroom settings during the middle and high school years. Those years were an academic dark tunnel for Eric and Eric really couldn't say that he much cared about the fact. Give him a basketball at the inner city park where he played pick-up for hours, or his 1950 Ford convertible to tinker with, and he was more than happy.

At that time of working with his doctor, moreover, Eric had just recently endured a grueling and traumatic death of a loved one, which when coupled with some other family stress points would seem enough to push anyone into depression.

He thought he had the answer. He needed pharmaceutical treatment for depression—an antidepressant. The problem was this: while talking with the doctor Eric never went into detail about the years of mood swings, the hypomania of writing all night and then working the next day, the awful drop into periods of loneliness, anger, and sadness. It was all solved by a magic pill. No one marveled at his recovery on Prozac more than he. The euphoria lasted four months, then began receding. It did so slowly at first, like a barely discernible waning of the tide, then with greater rapidity. What was it like to experience this?

Picture an even line—it may be a smooth biking path, perhaps a highway. That's the starting point for a normal person's life. Of course it has twists and turns, a few ripples, maybe even a pothole or two. Any life has its tension points and tragedies. None of us escape pain.

Now imagine that the path has some significant dip in it, so low you can't even see the main path from its bottom. You just have to keep working through it, walking along until you find the main path again. Sometimes one requires the aid of medication, but as time passes the main path is usually accessible again. For most people suffering from what is called "unipolar" or "clinical" depression, this provides a fairly accurate picture of the disorder: dips down into valleys of despair and anxiety, and an ongoing effort to regain the equilibrium of a "normal" life.

In bipolar depression, however, no "normal" path exists. We're in hilly country, even mountainous terrain now. At the depressive pole, one sinks like a rock into valleys that seem impossibly wide and deep, simply because he *has* been on the mountaintop.

Now picture the bipolar reacting adversely to an antidepressant—not an uncommon event. This one doesn't stop at a plateau on the way up; he simply jolts electrically to the summit. He dances where others fear to climb, feet clicking lightly on a thin sliver of rock that holds his head in the heavens.

But then—he always must—he trips while dancing and plummets down. Through clouds that darken around him. And the falling goes faster precisely as it goes further. Newtonian laws are suspended; no friction, no resistance, slow the plunge. And he lands not on a valley floor but in a swamp where the water is green-scummed and the sides steeply banked in rock, and the best he can do is swim hard, hoping he doesn't sink all the way.

There's a picture that will do as well as anything.

Constant reminders tell people enduring mental disorders that their lives will never be the same—that they will never be "normal." One such reminder is the need for blood tests that necessitate unending trips to the lab. On one Saturday morning in December, at 7:15 on dark streets, Eric headed to the blood lab housed in an inner city hospital. For weeks he and his doctor had been following blood trails into that strange terrain of "therapeutic levels." The term seems to mean little more than this—if it's going to work, this is the amount where it's likely to work.

Eric customarily had his blood tests taken during the week. Thursdays work well. He arrives at the lab five minutes before the door opens and is usually first in line. The personnel work quickly and professionally. The clientele look like people from any walk of life. Just a normal, everyday bloodletting.

This hospital resides in another world. Ruined husks of old buildings with grimed windows line the streets. People walk with stooped shoulders. Two blocks farther west are the cardboard shanties under the highway overpass. Litter blows randomly and no one cares or bothers to clean up. If one were to drive down one of these streets, in the evening, one would begin to wonder who all these people are, even as one locked the car doors. Monday through Friday these people can all go to a nearby clinic for health care.

What Eric did not know is that on Saturday mornings, if they have missed visits at the clinic, they come to the hospital. They come early when it's a cold day. By 7:30 the waiting room is half full. Eric files his forms with the receptionist. She tells him there's a slight delay; the technician couldn't get her car started. He sits on one of the hard plastic chairs, the kind where you have to slide through a half dozen angles to find any kind of comfortable position.

He picks up a magazine. *Highlights for Children.* He reads it anyway, quickly. A very large woman sits next to Eric. She eats little black things that look like licorice out of a bag in her purse. "That's a good one," she says. Eric raises the *Highlights* questioningly. She nods.

He is one with them. Certifiably. The blood order this time reads for lithium and depakote. They are playing a tennis match inside his head to see which one wins.

The man across from Eric sighs wearily. "Eight o'clock," he says to no one in particular. "Rolls around the same time every day." The woman next to him nods her head as if confronting a Kantian postulate.

But then Eric stops to think about it. What if eight o'clock didn't roll around the same time every day?

The technician, due thirty minutes ago, has her own concept of time. She walks in at 8:05, calls the first name, and the queue moves forward. Eric leaves at 9:12. On weekdays this process, start to finish, takes about 20 minutes. He wouldn't have missed this Saturday for the world. He now has friends all over. He finds himself checking his watch whenever eight o'clock rolls around.

At those times when the clock seems all wrong, like Alice in Wonderland, persons with mental disorders recite reasons for hope like clinging to a life raft and in time the pharmaceuticals that managed his illness did permit him the mental clarity to reflect. Here are some ways Eric began to search for hope, none of which has been easy. He doesn't set these forth as any surefire answers or "steps to wholeness." They are simply some lessons he appropriated during his own seismic swings through bipolarity.

The first, and most important, of these is to accept the fact that the myth of the normal male is precisely that—a myth. Somehow males have convinced themselves of some godlike figure of masculinity they must all aspire to. Many cultural gender distinctions of our fathers—grown men don't cry, etc.—have been broken down. But men have still placed iron walls around any indication of mental illness. They sneak into the psychiatrist's office after hours. They deny themselves, both their need and who they are. Look at any bookstore. While literally dozens of books about depressive disorders among women and written by women ripple across the shelves, very few about men written by men appear. One of those few is William Styron's groundbreaking work, *Darkness Visible*, where he describes depression as a "brainstorm" where sanity shipwrecks.

In the depressive phase, the illness itself speaks deceitful words into the mind of the person, telling him he is worthless, that he fails to match up to cultural expectations of manhood, that he dare not admit his weakness or seek help. Consequently help is often not sought. Eric learned the hard way that he couldn't grit his teeth and fight this illness out. He fought too long and too hard and got punished as a consequence. Here are the words of the first lesson: "I have learned since that I have an illness, and I will treat this illness with dignity and respect, but I am not the illness that I have." No more so, perhaps, than a man with a broken leg is himself a broken leg.

Second, Eric learned his weakness. Only two and a half weeks into his use of drugs for bipolar disorder, intended to stabilize his moods, his concentration and stamina under the new drugs had so deteriorated that, for the first time in his career, he had to take a medical leave of absence. He also had to understand that the course of the rest of his life would now be different as he acknowledged the reality of his weakness.

Once again, however, one's own incapacity to perform the most basic tasks of one's livelihood conflict with the cultural myth of male as achiever. It isn't only that the myth expects them to be diligent, dependable wage-earners, but also that they are expected to forge steadily ahead. Advancement and promotion bestow self-affirmation. When that very livelihood is jeopardized, and when the projected hopes of advancement either fall into question or vanish altogether, the diminishment of one's self is catastrophic.

Eric's task, during his recuperation, was to disengage his sense of identity from the cultural myth that "I am what I do." The task is especially daunting because the bipolar depressive has to strip away the masks by which he has presented himself to the world to fulfill that myth. Bipolar disorder is a world fabricated by lies; the first step toward reclamation of an authentic self is to strip them away. Like peeling away layers of heavy clothing, one has to say: These are the wrongs I have done. I am sorry for them. These are the things I can no longer do. These are the things that I must focus on, right now, to know myself. In this stripping away action, which is also a peeling away of certain cultural myths of masculinity, the bipolar's word to live by will become "No." Someday, if he says it often enough, he may relearn how to say "Yes."

The third lesson Eric undertook was an investigation. It was signaled in those fearful words of confusion that he threw at himself during the summer months: "I don't feel like myself anymore." The question, in its simplest form, is, "Who am I?" It is the necessary rebuilding process after the stripping away action of lesson two. The answers are much harder than Eric ever thought, even with helpful professional therapy. He is a man with a serious illness, who, with the help of psychotropic drugs, can nonetheless hope to function fairly normally. That is a fundamental reality he has to live with for the rest of his life. But it is so woefully partial—like picking up a twig and proclaiming that I hold a maple tree in my hand.

Eric, like each one of us, had to discover himself as a spiritual being, and that this biochemical malady in his brain in no way diminishes his spiritual worth. This world swarms with people who are convinced that mental disorders are a direct consequence of something someone has done wrong. While that may be true on some occasions (e.g., drug abuse), as an exclusive claim it's heinous. At a moment when, by virtue of the illness itself, the person feels guilty, such suspicions are the last thing he needs.

Eric, like each one of us, is relearning every day what it means to be a spiritual being. When he now asks himself who he is, he finds only one satisfying answer: "I am a child of God."

Eric, like each one of us, also has to put new images into the mind by an act of will. Like this one—on his office wall hangs a crude crayon drawing on yellowed paper. If one looks really close and carefully, I'm sure that one can tell it is a figure of a person. Stick arms rise from the tops of imagined shoulders. Beneath a bulbous body, like an egg on end, protrude two spectacularly squiggly legs. Sometimes Eric still feels like that person. But underneath it are some random scribbles and marks. He remembers the day his youngest daughter handed that drawing to him. He asked her what the scribbled marks said. "I love my daddy," she said.

As I reflect on experiences with mental illness in the lives both of friends and also of family members, I find that I have to retract some charges I made earlier in this study. They, basically, accused people who use such phrases as "finding joy in pain" or "the blessing of pain" of not taking the fundamental gravity of pain seriously enough. While I still recoil from such phrases with the jolt of an electric shock, I confess that my own experience with mental disorder has become a very odd sort of blessing. For I too am one of those who attempted to hide a mental disorder way too long, thinking it the "manly" thing to do. I too have had to learn to adjust to the daily use of psychotropic drugs, on a clockwork schedule. I too have learned that I have an illness that cannot be cured, but can be managed in such a way that I can live quite happily indeed. I too have learned that I have an illness, but I am not the illness that I have. The paradoxical discovery is simply this: suffering may, in its own strange way, be a blessing. More odd still, blessings are things we are thankful for. Even when we say "no" to the suffering, we might be thankful for the blessing.

Why is this? I go back to the initial proposition of this chapter. Mental illness still remains one of the most mysterious and least understood of the body's pains. By trying to understand myself, a necessary step toward my own recovery, I have gained more understanding of the pain of mental illness in others. I most assuredly do not mean I can lecture on brain chemistry, give psychological advice, or insert just the right words for encouragement. What I mean is that I can be there for others enduring the pain. I can listen, as long as necessary, and don't have to say a word of learned advice. I am said by my students to have "good ears." That's when they can say what they need to and it never passes out my lips as gossip or idle chatter.

Blessing others in such a way, with openness, honesty, and concern, in turn shapes a great blessing for me. My illness has not cast me aside from the human race; it had given me another way of entering into it more intimately than I would have ever guessed.

The second blessing is that I have grown closer to Jesus. I missed things before. I had always seen him more as God; now I see him also as fully human. I see his weariness, when he had to draw aside to pray and renew himself. I see his haunting loneliness as he prayed in the garden before his death. Even his own disciples couldn't stay awake to support him. I see his emotions, in his proclamations of love and even in the short verse: "Jesus wept" (John 11:35).

With my own illness fairly well managed now through effective medicines, a very careful life plan organized with my doctor, and the support of loved ones, I almost wonder if I might have missed these blessings otherwise.

For those afflicted with the pain of mental illness, or who know well someone who is, I feel obligated to raise one more, very uncomfortable issue. Here is the fact first: many people under the torment of a mental illness choose to take their own lives rather than suffer the pain a moment longer. Devastating consequences follow that action.

First, family and friends often wonder if they couldn't have done something more to prevent it. We have to remember that mental illness is an illness of the brain that not always affects external appearances. Sometimes we don't even know it's there. Certainly a trained professional can detect the physiological as well as behavioral signs, but by and large the person doesn't walk around with a sign hanging from the neck proclaiming his or her distress.

Second, sometimes the mentally ill person refuses to seek professional help or refuses to take prescribed medicines. Any professional psychiatrist or psychologist will work long and hard with a patient to put in place a rational plan to say no to the emotional urge to end the suffering by ending one's life. Furthermore, the wide array of medicines at the doctor's disposal can, over time, manage the illness. We don't speak of a "cure" here; there is none. But the illness can be managed, just as diabetes or kidney failure can.

The third implication involves those left behind. These thoughts nag the mind: What could I have done differently? And how do I know this loved one is in heaven? That second question is particularly contentious in Christian circles.

Some people take a very extreme and literal view of the commandment: "Thou shalt not murder" (Deut 5:17), understanding it to mean that one may never take the life of another. Yet, we know well that the commandment cannot be taken that specifically, for a chapter later in Deuteronomy we find the Israelites ordered by God to drive out all the nations and to "destroy them totally" (Deut 7:2). As we study scripture closer, "murder" seems to involve taking the life of an innocent victim. It is an act of violence against someone who does not deserve violence.

I believe the point is germane to the victim of suicide. Given his or her mental condition, the suicide is both aggressor and victim. But what exactly is the aggressor? It is the mental illness itself, the liar who tells the person that he or she is no good, or that the world would be better off without them.

Finally, there is an attendant question, following closely on the careful steps we have laid here. I am sometimes asked whether a mentally ill person who ends his or her life can go to heaven. I have no firm theological basis for answering this, but only the guide of logic. Review the propositions. The mentally ill person who commits suicide is at once the agent and the victim. That person did in fact take the life of him or herself. The mental illness, however, is the aggressor—that "thing" (act, event, or wrong)—that precipitated the action.

Furthermore, if that person ever had a saving knowledge of Jesus Christ, I firmly believe, without qualification, that that person will be rejoicing with his or her Savior beyond this life. Moreover, if under the influence of the mental illness, the individual appeared to deny the Savior, departed from fellowship with fellow believers, and seemed to take up fellowship with the world, I believe that individual's name will still be called in heaven, and that he or she will be seated at the throne of the glorious king in whom all things are made well and by whom all pain disappears forever and ever.

Mental illness is as much a bodily pain as my son's broken arm. Regrettably, since it occurs within the myriad intricacies of the brain, some people are quick to dismiss its severity and gravity. Although medical science can now demonstrate how depressive disorders work biochemically, along with such grueling companions as anxiety, panic attacks, and others, this is still the mysterious language of code words to the average layperson. It is easy to turn away from what we don't understand. The situation, however, is not one of our understanding the chemical compositions and their perilous passage through the brain. Rather, our role is that of the intercessor: lifting the person's need before Jesus's grace and then bringing that grace to the person.

Chapter Five

"Hear My Prayer, Oh Lord"

Spiritual Pain

REMEMBER HOW WE SANG our love songs for Jesus when we were children? How about "Jesus Loves Me," or "Jesus Loves the Little Children"? We even had our own special Advent song, "I Love Thee, Lord Jesus, Asleep on the Hay." How wonderfully uncluttered our lives were. We could truly live in the joy of the moment.

We didn't really leave those songs behind as we grew into adults. Those songs are like a cradle whose familiar and gentle rhythms confirm our faith. Somehow, they are still part of us, even as other hymns served as our vocabulary for love.

Sometimes our grown-up hearts are more troubled, though. How do we know Jesus loves us? Remember that first song listed above? It has the line: "For the Bible tells me so." Yes, it does. The Bible unwraps all the splendid story of Christ's love for us. Yet, deep inside, I may have the haunting feeling—How do I know Jesus loves me?

The second question is cousin to it—How does Jesus love us?

As I write this, I am at a familiar spot. Throughout the summer months I keep a chair and a round table under the birch tree in our backyard. Our aging Sheltie lies sprawled in the sun, twitching his ear every so often. This summer has been sweet to the flowers and they celebrate all around me. Blue morning glories cascade over the fence like a blanket. I can sense the glory of the Lord in this sun-dazzled world.

Yet, at this very moment, someone wonders if God loves him or her. They feel alienated and lonely. They feel a spiritual pain that cuts to the quick. Some plead, from the depths of their hearts, I just need someone to talk with me.

For quite some years now, Pat has volunteered with Meals on Wheels to deliver meals to the elderly and shut-ins. On her first day she was given a route through one of the most impoverished and gang-ridden sections of the city. It seemed also that every person she called on was in some desperate need or stage of pain. I went with her once, not too long after she started. I confess that I was more intrigued with the physical details of the hard-up landscape than the people. It's pointless to describe most of the homes, though. They stood in varying degrees of dilapidation, but in uniform degrees of desperation. This is where loss of hope was made tangible. It stood on warped clapboards and broken windows.

Some stand out. A young girl opened the door of a ramshackle yellow house to a foyer full of partially clad young children and the arched backs of, it seemed like, a million and six cats. There was the garage converted into an apartment where the blind lady lived. At another house we walked around to the backyard where the neighbor's two pit bulls jerked at their chains and growled like Sherman tanks.

More intimidating than the pit bulls was a ladder-like contraption hanging down from the second-story roof. The old couple's apartment had, in fact, been built into the attic through the second roof. I thought I'd stay down and play with the pit bulls. But I climbed, squeezed my eyes shut, and held my breath all at the same time. Then the bad part started. We had to cross the roof on some rickety wooden thing to a squalid hovel opened by a nearly naked person. No wonder—waves of fetid 90 degree air fell out, nearly knocking me off the roof. Then there is that final problem we should have learned when we were kids climbing trees. If you climb up, you have to climb down. Either that or move into a tiny dark box.

For me, I readily admit, it was a geographical tour. I wanted to see where Pat would be going. Not that I worried about it. She had worked in some very hazardous and threatening situations before. Besides, she has a card on her window visor that says "There Are Always Two People in this Car." One is this slim little 5'6" woman I married; the Other made the universe.

For Pat, however, Meals on Wheels developed profound spiritual ties that can only be broken by death. She spends time with a half dozen or so people, listening to their needs and praying for them. I can't wait to hear her stories over supper on Meals day. One of my favorite persons, whom I'll call Gracie, was virtually incapacitated by diabetes, her extremely large weight, and a half dozen complications. Gracie was a woman of sorrow and from whom men turned their faces. No one esteemed Gracie. Not only did

Pat have to spend extra time with Gracie, and do a whole lot of praying, but there were two unique events at Gracie's house.

Gracie didn't wash often. Her hairstyle was a long white towel wrapped turban style around her hair. The same towel, week after week. Nonetheless, Gracie insisted upon giving Pat a "bop," or kiss, every time she came. One day Pat was down with a bad cold, but Meals couldn't find a substitute so she did her route anyway. When she told Gracie that she couldn't bop her, the large woman began weeping. "I have to, Pat. If I don't bop you, then there's nobody else." A second element marked Gracie's stop as unique. After a few months Gracie would slip a piece of paper—her shopping list—into Pat's hand. Special things that Gracie wanted: milk, an ox tail for soup, pig knuckles, fruit. With a long series of deliveries, Pat sometimes didn't have time. Gracie understood, she appreciated the many times Pat did shop for her. She gladdened our hearts by never offering to pay anything.

Gracie died a few months ago. We read the obituary with surprise. She was years younger than Pat would have guessed. But, oh, how she missed that sanctified woman who would shout out, "Come here and let me give you a bop."

Sometimes one's spiritual attitude can overcome the afflictions of physical pain. We have all heard stories of people suffering terribly who glorified God with every last breath. Throughout the history of the church, people have died horrible deaths with the praise of Jesus on their lips. I don't know if I would have courage like that. I do know that many more people have experienced spiritual pain, feeling that they have been abandoned by God and that they are afflicted with some disease that roots in the soul.

Unless their hearts are shaped from granite, nearly every human since Adam has suffered occasions of spiritual pain. But how do we define it? It helps to put spiritual pain in context for a minute. Physical pain is fairly concrete. It hurts, and almost always we can point to the precise point of origin. Let me give an example from close to home—our kitchen. Often a hubbub of noise and a carnival of activity, Pat somehow orchestrates the processional with amazing grace. Especially so when we have groups of friends over for dinner. On this particular occasion it was Thanksgiving, when we alternated having one side of the family over year by year.

Pat was in the kitchen slicing carrots like a bandit while I was arrang-ing furniture. We have a good arrangement; she prepares all the food while I clean up the mess afterward. Probably there is more to it than that. I think Pat remembers my father, who stood side by side with my mother, both in aprons, preparing a dinner. Dad smoked a pipe, overloaded with tobacco like a wallowing ship, and with a ferocity seldom seen. As clouds of tobacco smoke ascended, a litter of ashes descended on the apples he was slicing into the pie. If he dropped a slice of apple, it went right back into the pie. Unless the dog got it first—a gourmet chef he wasn't.

I must say that I didn't think anything of this culinary waywardness when I was growing up. If a sibling took a swig of milk from the bottle and put it back in the refrigerator, I wouldn't have thought anything of it. In my wife's household they used glasses, and rinsed them afterward. They wouldn't be used again until they were washed. I'm fairly certain that Pat wanted me out of the kitchen for that very reason, even though I have since demonstrated that it is not a genetic trait. Nonetheless, she prefers me out of the kitchen. Until cleanup.

So it was on that Thanksgiving as I moved chairs and tables in the living room, also cleaning out the stock of toys that our children had hidden under them. (Why do children believe that under the sofa is the best toy drawer in the house?) Suddenly I heard a yelp from the kitchen. Pat called me with an urgency I hadn't heard before. And no wonder. That razor-like paring knife had nearly severed the tip of her index finger. We wrapped the finger tight in a towel that was soon soaking through. I called my oldest son, who had just gotten his driver's license, to take Mom to the emergency room. Pat had made it clear to me that she wasn't going to let this break up our Thanksgiving plans. In fact, she said, you're going to finish the vegetables. Such trust.

Such is a minor example of physical pain. Something rudely interrupts a normal bodily process, we emit a yelp, or a groan, or tears. For all the neuroscientific explanation of physical pain, spiritual pain appears to be yet more complex, for it occurs in a place where many scientists, as well as others, deny its very existence—the human soul. Yet spiritual pain is nonetheless real, nonetheless devastating. And although it demands spiritual answers, we are well aware that it affects the whole psychological and physical make-up of humanity as well. The fall of humanity may have scarred God's creation, but it also scarred humanity itself.

What is Spiritual Pain?

Perhaps it would be wise to address this issue first: What do we mean by the human soul? The issue is important simply because this is the place of spiritual suffering, a uniquely human property placed in our created being by the hand of God. Many of our age deny the very existence of the soul. Their first response might be: If I can't see it, it doesn't exist. We call this view empiricism—the only reality is that reality apprehended by the senses. There are all sorts of problems with that view. For example, just a moment ago I had glanced out of my window because birds were feeding on the fruit of my mountain ash tree. As I turned my attention back to my desk, does that tree cease to exist?

The more difficult view has to do with assumptions. In this case someone might say that I have never seen a soul; therefore, I cannot say that a soul exists. The problem is that all of us make assumptions that guide our thoughts and our actions. Listen to astrophysicist Meg Urry of Yale University: "Dark energy makes up two-thirds of the universe—and we don't know what it is."[1] There's an assumption as big as the universe. We all make such assumptions, every day.

The Christian framework works like this. We presuppose there is a God. Moreover, we accept that we know his nature and will through his revelation in scripture. His nature is Lord, Creator, and Redeemer, among others. His will is that we enter a loving relationship with him. How do we know this? Through his revelation, explicitly in two places.

The first of these occurs in the great Shema, the liturgical prayer recited by Jewish males and based on Deuteronomy 6:4–6: "Hear, O Israel: The Lord our God, the Lord is one. Love the Lord your God with all your heart and all your soul and with all your strength." This command is repeated a number of times in the Old Testament. In the New Testament, Jesus validates his Father's revelation, but with a slight twist: "'Love the Lord your God with all your heart and with all your soul and with all your mind. This is the first and greatest commandment'" (Matt 22:37; see also Mark 12:30, Luke 10:27).

Soul, then, differs from mind, our rational intellect; from strength, our commitment in deeds to God; and from heart, our deep conviction and love for God. Soul is where and how we experience God personally. The soul is also the seat of awareness that we have wandered from God—this mysterious thing called a conscience.

The soul is our intrinsic inner nature, the being God has crafted to commune with him in love. When we pray to God, our minds may shape the language, our hearts the devotion and praise, our strength the

---

1. Urry, "Dark Energy," 4.

commitment. The soul unifies these in communion with the Holy Spirit. Conversely, by the soul God communes with us. The fall in Eden may have clouded that link, but it has never severed it. The soul is at once the source of spiritual praise and also spiritual pain.

Spiritual pain may be said to take on three forms: guilt, alienation or forsakenness, and loneliness. They are not neatly set into categories. They overlap and interlap. The net effect is a distancing from God, and a sinking into our own inadequate selves.

The first signal of spiritual pain is guilt. That regulator of our conscience persistently nags us: You have done this wrong. This violates God's sovereign will. The problem is that people set the regulator of their consciences at different levels. People whose moral values are dredged from under a rock might say: If it feels good, do it. Some people twist the laws just slightly to their own advantage, thinking something like, I'll feel a little guilt but I'll get over it. Or, sometimes, they say we have to break a few laws to serve a higher good. The sole authoritative guide for right action is God's word, not our own reason.

Some people feel that God's commandments place them in a straitjacket. You may have heard the line: These laws just came from some ancient time. They're no longer relevant in the modern age. Consequently, moral values become relative to the age and guilt is a much diminished thing. We seem to live in a culture comprised of victims, and it is very comfortable because it assuages that nagging whisper of guilt to a warm, comfortable buzz. Like a narcotic, the postmodern view of everyone as victims simply anesthetizes us to the reality of wrongdoing. It is possible to anesthetize the soul; it happens all around us by this relativism.

What good is guilt? It prompts us that something is wrong. It is like the edge of the paring knife slicing across the index finger. You don't want blood in your carrots. Guilt tells us when we have strayed from God. It is a gift, really, implanted there in the soul by God to prompt us that something is wrong in our relationship. God didn't initiate the separation; he wants us back. But sometimes guilt is easier to ignore than heed. Why? Because guilt means I have done something wrong, that I need to bear my shame instead of someone else, and that I have to ask forgiveness for the deed about which I feel guilty.

Guilt is a spiritual prompter that our relationship with God lies askew. Perhaps the foremost example of this in scripture occurs in the life of God's chosen king—David. But in his awareness of guilt and his confession of sin, David sets a pattern for us. Psalm 32 fascinates me. It sets off heart-throbbing praise against heart-saddening awareness of guilt, a condition I sometimes find myself in. I want to praise God fully; at the same moment I feel unworthy even to pray to him. David begins the psalm with a rhapsodic statement of truth:

> Blessed is he
> whose transgressions are forgiven,
> whose sins are covered (1).

Then he remembers the state he was in before he experienced this truth. God's hand, David says, was "heavy against me" (4). His strength flagged; his guilt afflicted him totally. But,

> Then I acknowledged my sin to you
> and did not cover up my iniquity.
> I said, "I will confess
> my transgression to the Lord"—
> and you forgave
> the guilt of my sin. (5)

The corrosive acid of guilt that sapped David's strength was wiped clean when he confessed his wrongdoing to God.

Our human tendency when dealing with guilt is either to deny it or to run and hide from it. We fear exposure, even to God. Before his eyes, we sometimes think, we are as insubstantial as fuzzy X-rays. Our inner selves lie there, transparent and embarrassing. It's like that old dream of walking into a crowded event and you discover you have no clothes on. The consequence when we try to hide our guilt from God, however, is alienation from him.

God wants us to come to him, warts and all. I don't think God cares at all about how you look, nor necessarily about what you have done. After all, his son Jesus came into this world to take your hand and lead you into a safer place. I would rather be transformed than conformed. I would rather be washed than wrung out. But this isn't our natural state of affairs. We try to tune down the guilt register in that conscience. All the while, we slip from grace.

Properly understood, alienation is the distance by which we separate ourselves from God's grace. An alien is someone without a fixed home, a wanderer, a stranger. Our government even uses the term to identify someone who does not legally belong here. In the case of spiritual pain, alienation is self-inflicted. If I see poison ivy, which I know all too well from prior experience, I would be something of a madman if I entered a patch and started pulling it up with my bare hands. I don't belong there. I know the results of going there. And I will suffer exquisitely for having gone there.

Like the case of the poison ivy madman, we still persist in going places we know we don't belong. And we suffer all the pain and indignity for having gone. Now, in the many instances in which I have contracted poison ivy— quite by accident each time—I have to rush immediately to my doctor's office for injections of cortisone. If I can get there quickly enough, I can allay the agonizing pain of this infection to which I am violently allergic. If I do not get there quickly, soon my whole body will suffer an indescribable reaction.

Use this as an analogy for alienation. Guilt tells us the source of separation. It prompts us toward spiritual action, specifically, seeking forgiveness. Failing to respond, we enter a state of alienation, a distancing from God, where our wounds fester and spread. Like poison ivy.

The third trait of spiritual pain follows closely upon guilt and alienation, and that is loneliness. How do we understand loneliness? It consists of many forms, but primarily loneliness is always a state of separation and isolation. Just as someone suffering physical pain endures it in a highly individual way—"This is my broken wrist and it hurts me"—so too spiritual loneliness springs from a devastating sense of separation profoundly situated in the human soul. Such was the exact position of David when he made his plea in Psalm 10:1: "Why, O Lord, do you stand far off? Why do you hide yourself in times of trouble?" The question is not unique. We have all had those moments in our lives when we feel that God is distant, standing far off, and abandoning us. Turn to one person in David's lineage. With his last breath from the cross, Jesus cried out, "My God, my God, why have you forsaken me?" (Matt 27:46). At that point, Jesus was burdened with our sin. As Jesus was forsaken by God, so our sin was forsaken with him.

In his great act of redemption—in fact, in his life of redemption—Jesus strikes me as a singularly lonely person. At times it seemed that his own disciples were strangers to him. Several times Jesus has to stop his discourse and say "Do you still not understand?" (Matt 16:9; see also Mark 7:18, John 13:12). When Jesus depended upon them the most, they fell asleep while he agonized in prayer, then they ran away after his arrest. Finally, when it came right down to it, Jesus was absolutely alone in his redemptive mission. As Son of God, and as abandoned by God, his was the only sacrifice necessary and sufficient from all eternity to assuage our loneliness. No earthly treasure or treasured person can touch our spiritual loneliness, and at a touch bring total healing.

We address the three symptoms of spiritual pain—guilt, alienation, and loneliness. It would seem simple to add the three curative agents—confession, return and forgiveness, and a renewed relationship with Jesus. Indeed, while these agents may be curative and right, in the complexity of the human soul they speak only part of the truth.

For example, most victims of abuse feel enormous guilt. They feel that somehow they have done something wrong to merit this vileness leveled upon them. Most feel dirtied, sullied beyond the grasp of redemptive grace. Similarly, one who feels alienated from God may have overwhelming questions and seem unable to find satisfactory answers. The loneliness might, for example, arise from the inexplicable experience of grief, where all sense of order and fittingness seem abandoned. Spiritual pain is not the time for didactic answers—"Do this and then . . ." Spiritual pain requires an action of the soul. God, who is ever faithful, has provided just such a pattern in his revealed word. Remember when Jesus prayed in the garden on the Mount of Olives, the night of his arrest? He cried out to his Father, several times, "Father, if you are willing, take this cup from me; yet not my will, but yours be done" (Luke 22:42). Jesus poured out his soul; he pleaded before God. He joined a long line of biblical figures in what is known as lamentation.

When we think of lamentation, we probably turn first to Jeremiah, the likely author of Lamentations. The book does set many of the hallmark traits of a lament—the exposure of heartfelt pain, the uncertainty of why he is suffering, and the appeal to God for deliverance. The lament, however, extends much more broadly than Jeremiah. It was deeply engrained in Israel's spiritual consciousness, both as an individual and corporate sacrament to restore a right relationship with God.

We seldom hear of the practice of lament in our contemporary churches. Two reasons account for this: first, as we have acknowledged earlier in this study, the expression of personal pain is often messy and disruptive. We feel we are intruding upon the neat, orderly lives of others. We feel that others cannot understand our personal pain anyway, so we bury it deep inside where it festers like an untreated wound. The second reason arises from a particularly vile distortion of Christ's teachings that rampages like a virus through many religious communities. I call this the Gospel of Success religion. And it is virulent. It teaches that good health and good wealth are the signs of spiritual well-being. God is just waiting to dump out of heaven showers of money into sanctified little hands. I imagine Mother Teresa shaking her weary head. More likely she pays no heed whatsoever, now walking as she is on streets of gold by the Sea of Crystal.

The effect of either is to turn one inward. If I bear pain I am isolated. If I struggle with ends that never meet, a dollar that doesn't stretch far enough, or a roof that leaks, then I'm just not good enough before God. At least not in the Gospel of Success. Where do I turn? Back to the beginning. Back to God, for "In the beginning was the Word, and the Word was with God, and the Word was God" (John 1:1). When all else fails, when pain is compressed hard into the isolated soul, the lament leads us to first things.

The biblical lament is comprised of several qualities. First, it is directed to God. Rather than a simple outpouring, it assumes a divine listener. This dynamic is based upon the promise of James who tells us to "Come near to God and he will come near to you" (Jas 4:8).

Moreover, the nature of the lament is deeply personal. There are no secrets between us and God. I bring forth items that God already knows, and I know he wants to hear it from me. Because of this intensely personal quality, the lament differs from all of our other liturgical prayers; it's between God and me now.

The third trait of the lament is confession, for there can be no restoration of the soul without that. The time for secrets is past now. Moreover, only when we confess our own sins are we in a position to ask questions of God and to seek his power to overcome sin.

The final stage of the lament is affirmation. We don't have to wonder if this was all worth the trouble. We don't have to worry about whether we got through, as if our soul had a kink in its cablevision to the source of power. In 2 Chronicles 7:14, God appeared to Solomon and said: "If my people, who are called by my name, will humble themselves and pray and seek my face and turn from their wicked ways, then I will hear from heaven and will forgive their sin and will heal their land." That act of humbling oneself is the act of the lament. We see ourselves as we are and bring that self before God for healing.

I suggested that many instances of the lament occur in scripture. Nonetheless, they appear in two distinctly different forms. Thus, we consider here distinctions between individual and corporate lament, looking first at the individual lament.

Disconsolation. Perhaps that word best describes Jeremiah. His state was beyond any consolation by earthly measures. He was profoundly disturbed by worldly injustice: "Why does the way of the wicked prosper? Why do all the faithless live at ease?" (Jer 12:1). In addition, Jeremiah was deeply troubled by the waywardness of God's chosen people. This priest Jeremiah looked out upon a broken world, viewing the moral disintegration of the Jewish kingdom. When Nebuchadnezzar began taking the Israelites into bondage beginning in 605 BC, Jeremiah must have believed that he had witnessed the ultimate chasm between God and his people. The chosen people were led off as slaves.

So it was that Jeremiah turns from his prophetic ministry to deeply personal intercessory pleading before God. The brief Book of Lamentations begins with an expression of sorrow for the fall of Jerusalem. For the Jews, Jerusalem was more than simply mortar and bricks. It was God's earthly city. At the great temple, God himself made his dwelling place. And now the city lay in deserted ruins.

The harder thing for Jeremiah to deal with is why God let this happen. Was it "fierce anger" at Jerusalem's waywardness? (Lam 2:3). But why to this extreme? Jeremiah ticks off the devastations of Jerusalem in a litany of horrors.

> In fierce anger he has cut off
> every horn of Israel.
> He has withdrawn his right hand
> at the approach of the enemy.
> He has burned in Jacob like a flaming fire
> that consumes everything around it. (2:3)

In chapter three, however, the prophet turns inward and lays his personal horrors before God:

> I am the man who has seen affliction
> by the rod of his wrath.
> He has driven me away and made me walk
> in darkness rather than light. (3:1–2)

Jeremiah suffers all the signs of spiritual pain. He is bereaved by guilt. He feels acute alienation from God. He feels forsaken and alone.

The later Greek dramatists gave a different name for this process of lament. When the audience sees great and terrible things happen on stage, it undergoes a catharsis, a cleansing of emotions. Yet, Jeremiah clings to something greater than mere cleansing in the lament. The lament leads somewhere: It is not simply to wallow in self-pity. The lament searches for God.

Jeremiah's testimony out of the lament carries all the more force for the very rude and hard work of the lament itself. In chapter three, he cries out:

> Yet this I call to mind
> and therefore I have hope:
> Because of the Lord's great love we
> are not consumed,
> for his compassions never fail.
> They are new every morning:
> great is your faithfulness. (3:21–23)

This testimony guides him to the end of this abbreviated book. Basically, Jeremiah says that if this is so, then here is what we must do. He then lists the varying ways that the Israelites must call upon the Lord, now with the assurance that God will hear them.

Many other individual laments appear in scripture. One thinks of Moses's oft-repeated laments over a "stiff-necked" people. One thinks of Job's prolonged lament, and the complete insufficiency of the answers given by his self-absorbed friends to assuage it. One thinks, furthermore, of David's penitential psalms. Finally, one thinks of Jesus's lament over Jerusalem: "O Jerusalem, Jerusalem, you who kill the prophets and stone those sent to you, how often I have longed to gather your children together, as a hen gathers her chicks under her wings, but you were not willing!" (Luke 13:34). The individual lament, then, is an expression of our personal sorrow and spiritual pain before God—who we earnestly believe can heal the condition.

The corporate lament, as its name suggests, is a group of people seeking reconciliation with God. An example occurs after the Israelites returned from exile to Jerusalem, a story told in the Old Testament books of Ezra and Nehemiah. The familiar story may be briefly retold.

In 605 BC Nebuchadnezzar led the first wave of captive Israelites to Babylon. Other removals followed, until only destitute scavengers and a few people hidden in caves were left. The entire political and spiritual structure of Jerusalem had been destroyed. However, God did not leave his people in captivity comfortless.

Among the very first exiles were Daniel and his three friends, who provided a powerful witness for God. About twenty years later, the fiercely brave and stunningly beautiful Queen Esther literally saved all her people from genocide. In 458 BC, Ezra led the first exiles back to Jerusalem. And in 445, fulfilling the 60 years of exile that Jeremiah had prophesied, Nehemiah arrived in Jerusalem and rebuilding commenced.

It was the task of Ezra and his men to rebuild the altar and the Temple. It constituted a powerful sign to the marauders about them: Here we take our stand. At the heart of it is worship to the Lord of Lords. Nehemiah's task was to rebuild the walls that would protect this holy place.

But the Israelites had one other important thing that set them apart from all the surrounding people and that gave them a clarity and power their enemies could not even dream of. Ezra had taken along the Law of Moses. The people gathered around Ezra, who stood upon a tall wooden platform. There in the middle-eastern heat, Ezra read for six hours a day, while all the Jewish men, women, and children stood to hear the words. As he read, the listeners began to mourn and weep. They understood full well how far short from God's law they had lived in exile. They lamented.

Nehemiah 9:1 puts it like this: "The Israelites gathered together, fasting and wearing sackcloth and having dust on their heads." Each element had special significance for the Israelites. Fasting denied oneself to draw closer to God. Wearing sackcloth represented denying an old way of life and also sorrow for the sins committed in that way of life. Sprinkling dust on the head symbolized a burial of that old life and a need to be resurrected to a new life.

Is that the end of it, though? Does the personal or corporate lament end in a shattered soul and hopeless groveling? Here lies the very heart of the lament—as we reach out in humble faith to God, he reaches out to us in restoration. The lament affirms God's love for us. In Nehemiah, Ezra does not leave the Israelites standing forlornly in the dust. Instead, he prays the Lord's richest blessings over them. He prays for God's compassion, his power, his deliverance, his presence. This is not just Ezra's prayer, however; it is every believer's prayer. It is our prayer to receive when spiritual pain is at its utmost. Through the blood of Christ, God can, will, and does heal our spiritual pain also.

Suppose that after cutting her finger deeply Pat had tried to get by with makeshift methods. Probably one could make do with some ointments and some bandages. Let's say that we took the easy way out. Instead of going for stitches, Pat just pulled the bandages tight, downed some ibuprofen, and got by.

Then suppose we stripped those bandages off a day later. They were feeling sort of warm and tight. Against the pasty skin the line of the cut had turned a purple hue. Worse, it seemed to curl back from the inside out rather than come together. It oozed from one corner as the skin plumped. Infection had set in, threatening more deeply than it did originally.

Basically, the cut had needed immediate, professional intervention.

Spiritual wounds are often like that. No, they probably won't appear in front of others like a grimacing purple sore. We arrange our own bandages over them. But they also grow worse there in hiding—festering and spreading. Sometimes they consume one's entire life. Turning our spiritual pain over to the Great Physician is not one bit less urgent than our need for physical care.

Chapter Six

The Shockwave of Grief

Emotional Pain

GRIEF IS LIKE SUFFERING a concussion.

The first blow sends one reeling, dizzy, and uncertain. And it comes so unexpectedly.

I used to manage a slow-pitch softball team. During warm-ups one night I was standing about six feet behind the first baseman, filling out the batting roster. I never heard the shout. I just felt the impact of the ball on the side of my head and went down in a heap. Apparently the catcher mistook me for the first baseman. Grief hits like that.

Even if you have waited by the bedside of your loved one for days, waiting the moment of dying, grief so rudely sends your life careening. In earlier chapters we made distinctions. Physical pain, psychological pain, and spiritual pain all have their unique properties. Grief seems to compound and encompass them all.

Grief is rude. It enters the house uninvited and unwanted. A burglar ransacking everything it can take. It kicks its hard boots up in the best table, leans back, and doesn't care about the destruction it leaves.

In his book *Lament for a Son*, Nicholas Wolterstorff, well known Christian philosopher at Yale University, writes of his son's sudden death in a mountain climbing accident in Austria:

> Something is *over*. In the deepest levels of my existence something
> is finished, done. My life is divided into before and after. A friend
> of ours whose husband died young said it meant for her that her

youth was over. My youth was already over. But I know what she meant. Something is over.[1]

Grief is like that. Like a sudden rip in the fabric of our lives. Life itself divides into before and after.

Grief always separates, fracturing a relationship. Few of us grieve when we step on an ant. The ant is completely anonymous to us; we have no relationship with it. More of us might grieve when a majestic, spreading maple tree is sawn down for a building project. The maple had no sentient relationship with us. It didn't know anything about us. Yet its absence may sadden us because some beauty that delighted us is now gone. We enjoyed the way it cast shadows on the meadow, the way its leaves tossed with silver light under the summer sun, the way those same leaves twisted like orange torches in the autumn. Something of majesty has disappeared from the earth.

It is fitting that we grieve such loss of natural beauty. Each time a harmonious order, like a very fine watch mechanism, is jarred out of synchronicity. But there are other trees. We take joy in them. In time we no longer think of the maple.

Our lives are filled with separations. A friend moves to another state, or a friendship somehow, inexplicably, just ends. A job that provided steady income is suddenly canceled; layoffs and "cost-cutting measures" sever us from a source of joy and stability. A tornado levels a high school, a hurricane devastates a city, a wildfire burns nearly a hundred homes. We grieve these events. Our lives are disrupted. We suffer separation.

All of these differ in degree of attachment. Most are totally detached from the demise of an ant, or say, a wasp or a bee. So many exist that their lives seem fairly expendable; in some cases, such as a colony of ants in your house, preferable. Some higher orders of animals, it seems, develop real attachments with humans, as do we with them. Even so, that varies by culture. Some people have pet pigs; others eat bacon.

We do appreciate God's revelation of natural beauty. We see in it the imprint of his original design, marvelous with both symmetry and diversity. We acknowledge that the task of Adam to be a steward of the earth falls to us also. Yet, I spray that patch of poison ivy by the back fence with the strongest weed-killer I can find. And it's hard to love crabgrass. We learn too soon that this world is fallen too.

Particularly so when we witness the series of what we call "natural disasters" that envelop the world. Unless we carry hearts of stone, we stagger

1. Wolterstorff, *Lament for a Son*, 46.

before the sheer number and magnitude of them. Earthquakes rock Japan, drought ravages Africa, tsunamis destroy miles of land and thousands of people. While we are saddened for the people who endure such massive death and destruction, unless we know particular persons among them, our sorrow is quite objective. We grieve in the abstract. We don't quite know what to make of it all and take refuge in the ordinariness of our own lives.

But our grief becomes powerfully emotional and deeply personal when the person we love has a loving relationship with us. That person may be a loving spouse of forty-seven years; it may be an infant of four days. That person may be a son or daughter who died in the flower of promise; it may be a son or daughter who lived longer than expected with some wasting illness or handicap. This we can't escape. This we care about profoundly. This startles and brings the tears of grief.

Such sorrow is relational. It involves us as a person, deeply, intimately bound in the personhood of another. That other person has affirmed us of who we ourselves are as persons. That close friend may have been the very one who encouraged our gifts, who gave us courage in time of need, or perhaps even had to point out some fault to us. I have sometimes thought of a close friend, marital or otherwise, as someone you can laugh with and not feel stupid, and as someone you can cry with and feel comfort.

These are the relationships with which God has graced our lives. They very much reflect the relationship we have with our Savior himself. When broken, the absence isn't an inconvenience. It questions everything we know about ourselves and about our love for others. Grieving people sometimes say, "It feels like I have a hole in my heart." Somehow, that isn't quite strong enough for human grief. It feels like you have a jagged, bottomless pit in your heart. And that you have just fallen into it.

Throughout history, humankind has grieved for that separation. It began when Adam and Eve were cast out of Eden. Something died there, irrevocably. A close relationship was severed. In *King John* Shakespeare wrote:

> Grief fills the room up of my absent child,
> Lies in his bed, walks up and down with me,
> Puts on his pretty looks, repeats his words,
> Remembers me of all his grievous parts,
> Stuffs out his vacant garments with his [grief's] form.[2]

So it has been since Eden. Grief sidles into the vacancy and lives there.

2. Shakespeare, *King John*, III. iv, 93–97.

Today the cemetery shines with beauty. Sprinklers sweep over the long stretch of emerald green lawn. To the south is a reflecting pond and a memorial garden to commemorate aborted babies. It is a healing garden, marked by stages through confrontation to forgiveness. Sometimes my wife and I walk its pathways. Dappled shade and the scent of flowers go with us. We all have something to confront and seek forgiveness for.

I am standing before the headstones of my parents. On Mother's Day we lay a spray of lilacs and tulips on Mother's grave; on Father's Day a single red rose on his. Next to their graves are the headstones of my aunt and uncle and one cousin. Before me, the sprinklers shoot long arcing sprays, the mist rising like rainbows in the sunlight.

To the north, only about fifty feet away, in a small cove sheltered by aged oaks, lies the children's cemetery. I walk there slowly.

The markers here are hard to find, circular bronze disks nearly lost in the play of shadows. I stop at the first one: Rachel Timmerman, my niece.

It is not a pretty story, but it has a happy ending. At the age of nineteen, Rachel had been convicted of a drug charge and did six months in jail. Shortly before her arrest, she had given birth to a baby girl, Shannon. The father's mother cared for the baby during the sentence.

We were unusually close to Rachel. She had often stayed with us as a young child. Blonde-haired, full of energy, she seemed to us the unlikeliest person to get caught in the drug world. Now, during the incarceration, Pat would not let the relationship die. A regular correspondence developed—long letters in which Pat affirmed both her own and Jesus's love for Rachel. In one letter, Pat asked if there was anything she could do. Rachel's response: Please send me a Bible. The last letter Pat received from Rachel reaffirmed her newly found faith in God. She was Jesus's child.

One can renounce a former way of life; it is harder to escape it. Before Rachel was charged and sentenced, a man from that former life brutally raped her. After she served her sentence, she was scheduled to testify against him at his upcoming trial.

She went out one evening with her baby, Shannon, and neither returned. Several months later Rachel's body was found in a small lake, chained to cement blocks, her mouth glued shut with duct tape. Shannon has never been found.

Several years later the psychopath who had raped Rachel and killed her was brought to trial, convicted, and sentenced to death. On the one hand, one can say that justice was served. But restoration can never occur. The separation is final. Or is it?

At Rachel's funeral the Bible that Pat had sent her lay atop the casket. I can't remember many of the words of that service, but I'll never forget that Bible lying there. Rachel knew those words—"I am the resurrection and the life. He who believes in me will live, even though he dies; and whoever lives and believes in me will never die" (John 11:25–26)—and death was not the end of the matter for her. Nonetheless, we mourn in this life because a living being whom we loved is no longer with us.

Grief is like a tightrope for the believer. We may have assurance of the beloved's eternal destination; in this life separation works like a raw wound in our spirits. It is ever so.

Sometimes separation comes naturally, the mortal body's own method of shutting down. Sometimes it enters suddenly, by accident, disease, or as in Rachel's case, by violence. Sometimes it slips into our most unexpected hours. I take one small step, and stop before another bronze disk: Rebecca Timmerman, the younger sister Rachel knew all too briefly.

Death sent no messages of warning, but simply crept in between the nine o'clock and eleven o'clock feedings so that Rebecca, laid to sleep warm and living, was picked up with the chill of death on her. My brother placed his lips on hers and tried to resuscitate her, his tears falling on her cold eyes, while the wail of sirens split the night.

He called me, at five in the morning, December 26, 1983. Just the day before, Christmas day, we had gathered together, passed Rebecca from arm to arm. What could we do now? We could be there, at the hour of need. While we struggled later that morning to write the obituary with the funeral director, we fumbled with the words. We followed the polite formulas. Rebecca Kay went to be with the Lord? No, say, went to be with Jesus, because she died on Jesus's birthday.

Born on October 25, 1983, Rebecca died on December 25, 1983. Those are the hard, unforgettable words that coil into the tissue of the brain.

There were only three cars at the cemetery, holding our entire family. The one who had left us, the youngest, Rebecca, rode in the station wagon that led us to this barren ground hallowed only by the gravesite. We tried to walk in the tire tracks of the tractor that dug the grave through the deep snow, cradling that small casket that my brother and I were carrying, stumbling and slipping toward the grave.

The December wind wailed out of the north, gray snow pelting and drifting in the streets, in the back reaches of the cemetery. Three feet of snow on the ground and the temperature hovering around zero for the second consecutive week. Winter starts hard and early in Michigan.

When we arrived at the gravesite we weren't sure what to do. The grave was so shallow, so small. Only four feet deep. The old man by the tractor asked if anyone had straps. No one did. It was better that way, for, by getting down on our hands and knees in the snow and dirt by the grave, each holding an end of the suddenly heavy casket, we were able ourselves to lean down and gentle Rebecca's casket home.

We thought of Rebecca's tiny form inside the white fiberglass, dressed in the pink sleeper that was her Christmas gift, her hand fisted around a spray of pink rosebuds. We saw her there, while the gray sky blew snow and the wind wailed at the tears on our cheeks. It was my sister-in-law who said that when Rebecca rose to meet Jesus, she would be holding fresh roses in her hand to greet him.

How could we not weep, seeing that.

With the wind breaking my words in pieces as I tried to pray, those in the family who had to wait stood around that tiny space beneath our feet, held hands, and said goodbye to Rebecca.

Our flower for two brief months. She flourished, blossomed, and then within seconds during her sleep, died.

We turn now from the grave, the frozen dirt clinging to our clothes and on the backs of our hands.

I do not know, when I see Rebecca again, how she will greet me. Will she be a young child romping on the playgrounds of heaven? Will she be a young woman, holding out to me a spray of roses?

This I believe, and it is a mystery too deep for words, but because of the fierce joy of the Lamb of God, who devoured death, I will most surely know it. Truly it is so. In that final separation we cling to the promise:

> Death has been swallowed up in victory.
> "Where, O death, is your victory?
> Where, O death, is your sting?"
> Thanks be to God! He gives us the victory
> Through our Lord Jesus Christ.
> (1 Cor 15:55–57)

Yet, we walk daily in a broken world. Death comes too quickly. Or, in some cases, too slowly. What do we do?

Separation is the pain of parting. It stings to the core. No one can produce a magic ointment to take the sting away. Nonetheless, we in the body of Christ have the honor, the high privilege, of modeling Christ himself to the grieving. We are, first of all, present. That can be the most critical element. The bereaved knows that he or she is not alone in this sojourn in sorrow. We walk alongside. Sympathy cards are appreciated. Funeral home visits invaluable. I know. During my own grieving I have needed others to grieve with me, to share my tears. Most often, however, the bereaved needs a human presence there in the abyss of loneliness. It is not the time to offer advice or our own woes; it is a time simply to be there, to listen, to understand, to pray.

The second way we model Jesus is through compassion. That is an interesting word. From the Latin roots, it means literally to suffer with. Sometimes mistaken for pity, compassion is active involvement. It is an act of setting aside our own needs and demands for those of another. How often we read that Jesus had compassion upon others. (See, for example, Matthew 9:36; 14:14; 15:32; 20:34.) That means he became one with their suffering.

Showing compassion, then, is a good bit more than saying, "I feel sorry for you." Compassion steers us out of our way and leads us to the point where the needs of others are greatest. The "others" here consist of more than the bereaved. They include the lonely, the lost and disenfranchised everywhere. Isaiah, prophet of God's justice, made it perfectly clear:

> He has sent me to bind up the brokenhearted,
> to proclaim freedom for the captives
> and release from darkness for the prisoners,
> to proclaim the year of the Lord's favor
> and the day of vengeance of our God,
> to comfort all who mourn,
> and provide for those who grieve in Zion—
> to bestow on them a crown of beauty
> instead of ashes,
> the oil of gladness
> instead of mourning.
> (Isa 61:1–3)

Isaiah thereby gives us an action plan for doing compassion. It is not difficult to find the need. Isaiah's list is all-encompassing of humanity and applies no less today.

The third way we model Jesus, providing comfort, can also be taken with deceptive simplicity. Like being present with the grieving person, like having compassion for him or her, comfort often is understood as a one-time action that at least leaves us satisfied that we have done our part. But like being present and showing compassion, providing comfort is a committed action, a dedication. It can consist of both helping the person and also getting help for the person to allay the emotional damage of grief.

Earlier in this book, I referred to my wife Pat's struggle with postpartum depression. Some of the emotional devastation arose from the fact that Pat had always been the strongest woman I knew, despite her petite frame. She has been gifted with unusual courage. Trained as a psychiatric nurse, she went bravely into situations most of us would avoid by a mile. When I was in Vietnam, drafted out of grad school, she found an apartment and worked night, double, and weekend shifts to make the time pass. One night she had to fend off a stalker at 1:00 a.m. For years she volunteered at an inner city clinic, treating the homeless and mentally ill who wander those streets. A strong woman, but especially in her Christian faith. Truly, she has been the lodestar in our spiritual life, mixing a rare gentleness with an absolute assurance of the authority of God.

Depression is a cruel guest. It throws questions and doubts at the ill person, trying to vacuum out every vestige of strength and faith.

But it is also a leering monster in the home of a father trying to raise three older children and a two-month old baby with lungs that could shatter crystal a mile away. I was not very good at the task.

Housekeeping was fairly easy. When I walked the baby at night in the living room, trying to soothe him with my warped singing, I systematically kicked loose books and toys under the sofa. Good. Clean. When Pat did her version of housekeeping later on, she nearly had to use a crowbar to pry the stuff out of there. I was, I might say, successful in keeping some order. I kept all the dirty dishes in the kitchen, teetering in piles across the counter.

Then there was this thing with the 1:00 a.m. feeding. Why he would want to eat in the middle of the night, I couldn't figure out. As I staggered out of bed, I realized it's more than food he wants. I call this the Midnight Express. Purple plums and cereal arriving at the station. Yikes! Somehow it leaked past the two diapers and rubber pants and saturated his sleeper. And the blanket and sheet. First things first. I strip Joel and the bedding and plop him in the tub. Oh, my, but he loves this. Maybe I could just prop him in the tub and leave him there a few weeks.

Okay. Now he has a wad of new diapers on. His middle looks like a basketball. The messed up clothes are in the diaper hamper—close to overflowing now, schedule it for 7:00 a.m. wash. Now Joel should be ready for bed, right? Of course not. All clean and cuddly, he wants to play. And there sit the miles of dirty dishes.

I set Joel in one of those plastic seats, strap him in, plug in a bottle, and put him on the floor. Then tackle the dishes. The hot soapy water feels good. I listen to the murmurs of pleasure behind me. Funny, I thought I heard the bottle drop to the floor. I risk a glance over my shoulder. There was Joel, happily gumming the dog's rawhide bone. Do you think I took it away from him? No way.

So it was our house veered on the edge of chaos. Every other day one of the grandmothers came over to try to make a dent in the cleaning and do some wash. (I did the cloth diapers with my own magic formula—a half cup of whatever I could reach on the laundry shelf.) During that time I took the kids to visit with Pat.

But I must confess that my life whirled like the outer edges of a tornado. Thanks be to God, others realized that I needed comfort and stepped in. Within days of Pat's hospitalization, a member of our church's care committee came over to arrange meals. Then my sister-in-law called one day and announced, "I'm taking Joel overnight. You need a break." A close friend of ours, with whose husband I played softball, came over and said, "You need to play softball tonight. I'm watching the kids. Stay out as long as you like." And so the offers came in. Even though it was summer, someone took over the house so I could go to my office for the day. Another friend took the older kids to his cottage for the weekend.

I received comfort. I also had to realize that I needed it. In times of stress and grieving, there is little room for the "stiff upper lip" syndrome. We can't do it all ourselves. Comfort, then, works two ways: being open to giving it, and being open to receiving it.

How remiss we would be if we failed to mention spiritual comfort also, for here lies the heart of our heart's healing. In the very presence of our desolation and the darkness of grieving, there comes divine consolation.

In an article titled "A Love So Fierce," Cornelius Plantinga, Jr., convincingly ties our human suffering to the suffering of Jesus. Sometimes, Plantinga argues, we fail to comprehend the urgent relevance of the cross to our own suffering:

> I know that the cross can be decorated in popular piety and domesticated and trivialized. Still, in suffering we need to turn toward the cross. For in the passion and death of Jesus we see the

same blend of inevitability and outrage that we see in our own; indeed, we see the very mold, the very prototype of it.[3]

At such a moment, Plantinga points out, Jesus's cry joins the cries of countless others who are pounded in the sea of suffering. Here is the prophetic fulfillment not only of Isaiah's words but also of the Christian plea: "Thus Jesus Christ bears our griefs and carries our sorrows. He was sharing the lot of all who cry half-devout, half-profane 'O my God!' when they are stabbed with the knowledge of death. He then shares the lot of those who nonetheless entrust themselves into the hands of a God who, as C. S. Lewis once said, 'knows how to do such fearful things with those hands.'"[4]

What is the meaning of Jesus' suffering, of the cross, then? Is it only the heartbroken cry? No. Plantinga observes that the cross is ultimately his sign of fierce love: "The cross of Jesus Christ—this ugly thing stuck up like a scarecrow in the center of our religion—tells us of a love so fierce, so determined . . . that its bearer is willing to be humiliated and tortured and bewildered and, for a time, to be dead."[5]

Yet we cry out, why hast thou forsaken me? We cannot understand why it happens to us: we want to see the light but the waves of darkness pound over us.

But does the darkness ever overpower the light?

The story of Job is incomplete until we read the song of Job, "I know that thou canst do all things, and that no purpose of thine can be thwarted" (Job 42:2).

The lament of David is incomplete until we read his hymn of joy. "Weeping," wrote David, "may tarry for the night, but joy comes with the morning" (Ps 30:5). The light will crash through the waves. Only hold on. God will not forsake you to the waves.

And the lonely cry of Isaiah, drowned out in the roar of confusion, is incomplete until we hear him proclaim God's promise that "They who wait for the LORD shall renew their strength, they shall mount up with wings like eagles, they shall run and not be weary, they shall walk and not faint" (Isa 40:31).

And Jesus? Forsaken? Bereft of the light and plunged into darkness? The Bright Morning Star seized from the heavens and plunged into the sea of human despair? The devil could not hold him. The darkness can never

3. Plantinga, "A Love So Fierce," 5.
4. Ibid., 6.
5. Ibid.

contain the light, for the darkness, by its very definition, is simply a deprivation of the light. It is dependent upon light for its very meaning. Without light, we would not know what the darkness is. And how can the darkness, then, hold the light of the world? A shattered grave, blasted apart by the light of all ages, is the testimony. In the gutted wreck of that grave lies the foot of the bridge out of all darkness.

That is where our hearts turn—to the light of the Bright Morning Star. But this we also know, and it is grim: that we walk through this life on a way plunged between perfect light and dark imperfection. So it will be until God's appointed time when darkness, grief, and sorrow are banished forever.

Chapter Seven

The Pain of the Prodigal

IN HIS GOOD NEWS *about Prodigals*, Tom Bisset writes that "faith rejection is more about searching for truth than it is about rejecting truth."[1] I'm afraid that Bisset may have stated the case too simply. I have long had an axiom about the students I teach at a Christian college. Basically I am afraid of two kinds of students: those who never have a question and those who think they know all the answers. Complacency and arrogance are twin threats to authentic Christian faith. We may all be truth-seekers, as Bisset suggests. That does not necessarily mean that prodigals are seeking truth, but so often it is upon a path of relativism and self-destruction.

While researching this chapter, I studied literally dozens of books and articles by authors writing from within the Christian faith. Some were as simplistic as to be nearly laughable—"If you do these steps, this will happen." In fact, you, the spouse, parent, sibling, friend of a prodigal, often feel virtually powerless before the danger. Some books tell honest, heartbreaking stories of personal pain. Some have happy endings, most don't. In a final category I find a number of personal narratives, memoirs if you will. Some of these, like Michael English's *Return of the Prodigal*, are bone-chilling accounts of personal loss.

However we engage this field of prodigality, whether by theory, research, or personal accounts, one thing remains: those people dealing with prodigal loved ones hurt. They grieve over a profound loss. They seek answers when their world is twisted askew. Prodigality is a disease; it's a cancer in the body of the church triumphant. It's an uninvited guest in the home that sits with his muddy boots up on the best table, sneering malignantly. Prodigality is the knife in the soul of the person, severing hopes and

1. Bisset, *Good News about Prodigals*, 12.

dreams, relations and religion. My belief is that prodigality is an addiction, a paralyzing addiction. My thesis is that this addiction occurs in the same relation one has with drugs, in relation to the world, and in relation to self. It manufactures prodigals.

The problem of any addiction is twofold. Before the first experience, one has no idea of the consequences. And after the first experience one can't go back to never having used. This will become clear in our discussion of three forms of prodigals today.

First, we have to ask what exactly is a prodigal. We can think of dozens of examples, from the prodigal son in Jesus's parable to the teenager who used to sit next to you in the church pew. The very word *prodigal* is a paradox, for it carries two contradictory meanings. On the one hand it suggests generosity to others; on the other to squander, presumably to meet selfish ends. The Latin *prōdigere* literally means "to drive away," as with others. We are considering here those individuals who have driven us away in order to serve their own gratification. That's how we understand a prodigal. He or she has turned away from traditions and values, has driven away our attempts to reach him or her, and has abandoned the fabric of our hearts and homes to gratify selfish ends.

I begin, then, with the abandonment into the world of drug addiction, for it seems to me all prodigality is an addiction that destroys sense and measure. We need those qualities to survive with others in a community.

If it hasn't occurred in your own family, it probably has in a family you know well. Addiction to drugs is pervasive, epidemic, and relentless in its search for new victims. Those who have studied addiction point to three primary causes: low self-esteem, peer-pressure, and dissatisfaction about present affairs with the need to experience new situations. Those can vary for, just as pain is experienced individually, so too the tumble into addiction is individual. The only sure rule of addiction is that if you never use for the first time, you'll never be an addict.

Furthermore, it is impossible to generalize about cultural, social, and ethnic circumstances. Addiction respects none of these. It invades the mansion on the far edge of town and the inner-city tenement. Rodney J. Mulder, Dean of the Social Work department at Grand Valley State University (Michigan), conducted numerous studies of drug and alcohol use in county-wide high schools. Among the disturbing findings were that there was little noticeable difference between schools in poorer districts, those in wealthy districts, and in public or Christian schools. Students are not drug-proofed by being in a wealthy or Christian school. The only significant difference appeared among those students who called themselves "religious." This designation, suggesting dedication to an orthodox faith, appeared in all three districts. These students were far less likely to use drugs.

Two of the most startling facts about drug use today are its ready availability and its relatively inexpensive cost. Appearances fool us. The most cherubic boy or girl in your high school may be dealing marijuana or cocaine. They may, even if they are using, be still maintaining relatively high grades. If not within the high school, it's readily available in any area of town. In my mid-size city of Grand Rapids, Michigan, I would say that I could procure a baggie of marijuana within thirty minutes, and most of that would be driving time.

Moreover, procuring a single use amount is not very expensive. Marijuana, in my city, is generally sold by the "baggie" or a single gram, for 10–20 dollars, depending on supply. An "eighth," or 3 ½ grams, of marijuana costs $50. Cocaine is sold by the gram or half gram at 50–100 dollars. Crack, commonly called "rocks" or "stones," is sold in multiples—one for $10, five for $50, ten for $100. Heroin, which is increasing in popularity, sells by the gram or "pack" for $100–225 each. While not large figures, the unseen calculation is that the user constantly needs to increase usage as the addiction deepens. At that point an overnight binge on cocaine can easily cost a thousand dollars.

Like all addictions, drug addiction is progressive.[2] Use of alcohol and marijuana begins as early as middle school, among the 11–12 year age group. The pattern intensifies in usage and amount into high school, where, in the eleventh and twelfth grades, powder cocaine is introduced, often by a dealer in the school selling to support his or her own habit. Crack cocaine, a hardening of the powder with the addition of baking soda and water into a "rock," generally isn't introduced until the user is 18–21 years of age. These four—alcohol, marijuana, powder cocaine, and crack cocaine—are the primary addictive drugs used by our young people today. Singly or collectively, they create a cycle of increasing need, dependency, and desperation to get more. In the final analysis, there is no such thing as "recreational"

2. See Walton-Moss, *Substance Abuse*. This authoritative and up-to-date textbook is part of the curriculum for continuing education for medical professionals. In plain and direct language the text examines the nature and use of major drugs, with methods of treatment, and makes use of the more recent national surveys. This is my primary source for statistical and evidentiary information.

or "casual" use for a drug addict. Either you use and you're an addict, no matter how well or how long you disguise it, or you don't use and you are not an addict.

The numbers of drug addicts are so prevalent in our nation, and the rate of successful treatment so slim, that virtually everyone knows of an addict in the immediate family, among close relatives, or in the church community. The only problem is—they have disappeared. Increasingly possessed by their disease, the addict is ashamed to be in company he or she formerly felt comfortable with. If the addiction is severe and treatment unsuccessful, they may be forced out of the family unit. It can reach the point, and often does, where parents, for example, have to close their doors against a son or daughter. This is the hardest act parents of prodigals may face, yet there is biblical precedent and injunction for this action.

If there are multiple causes for addiction, as we saw earlier, so too the effects extend beyond disappearance from the home, either self-imposed or by the actions of another. Drug addicts, in moments of sobriety, will talk honestly about the guilt and shame they feel. While many drugs physiologically induce a state of post-euphoric depression, the depression doesn't lift when the addict is clean and sober. Some drugs, such as cocaine, work so powerfully on key neurotransmitters that they lead to long term clinical depression.

Drug addiction, nearly all professionals agree, is a disease. That may be so, but it begins with a choice. Individuals are responsible for the consequences of their choices. In the case of drug addiction, the illicit drug often leads to illegal behavior, most notably in this case by dealing, or by theft, or by sale of belongings to support the habit. Young people especially, as opposed to long-time and chronic users, know their actions are wrong—morally, socially, psychologically, and spiritually. At once this knowledge increases their painful experience of guilt and shame. They live in another world, having abandoned the traditions of their first world.

If we are to see drug addiction as symptomatic, or as a common basis, for any addiction that leads to prodigal behavior, it is time to summarize some of the qualities we have been investigating. Causes of the addiction vary but commonly include low self-esteem, peer pressure, and dissatisfaction with things as they are. An example of a varied cause would be a form of self-medication for such psychological problems as depression, hyperactivity, or inattentiveness. We have seen, secondly, that the addiction is progressive, requiring larger amounts to achieve the desired effect. Finally, we have noted the effects of the addiction: the personal pain of guilt, shame, anger, depression, and separation.

In any case of addiction, however, it is not the addict alone who suffers pain. In particular, spouses and parents suffer acutely. It goes beyond the deep hurt of having a loved one abandon us for an addiction that has taken over their lives and made them a different person than we ever knew before. The pain moves beyond that to a number of different issues that collectively leave our world in unbearable turmoil. I observe just a few of what I would call psychological, physical, and spiritual reactions.

The first, psychological, is the process by which we call into account our own performance as parents or spouses. The normal reaction to a prodigal is great sadness, but following upon that a questioning of ourselves to determine what we did wrong to cause this. It is an inevitable process because none of us is a perfect parent or spouse. We have all bitten the apple of original sin. To show that our only deliverance is through Jesus, Paul wrote at length in Romans 5 of how all have sinned. He didn't list any exceptions. We are all, then, aware of our own imperfections as parents and spouses. Furthermore, we tend to see our children as reflections of ourselves, for better or for worse. The frequent psychological reaction to prodigals, then, is where did *I* fail? What did *I* do wrong?[3]

The painful consequence of this part is a constant second-guessing of ourselves. Since I don't use my tools much anymore, I often hang out with my young grandson in my tool room where I let him exercise his imagination with some tools and scrap lumber. He started simply—drilling holes or pounding nails into wood, for example. This past week he got into a project. I was in the next room listening to his humming and whistling, the drill singing, the hammer whacking. After quite some time he came out with his finished product. I recognized it immediately—a picture frame—albeit made from 1x6 boards of unequal lengths with enough screws in it to endure an earthquake. I praised him profusely, and it was really quite good. "It's a little bit crooked," he said, "but I sure tried." Sometimes that's the best that we parents and spouses of prodigals can say.

Let me reiterate that my larger purpose here is to analyze or diagnose the problems of pain, and not to suggest solutions that often are too superficial or simplistic. And I should reiterate my reason for this: pain is

---

3. It is not my place here in this analysis to provide answers to all the questions I raise. In this case, however, I do recommend the book *Family Fears*, by Schruer and Schruer. See also *Prodigal People*, by Knoll and Hawkins.

always experienced individually. There are no universal cure-alls or treatment plans. This also holds true in dealing psychologically with prodigals. Nonetheless, I'm compelled to raise a few biblical instructions in such situations. In 2 Corinthians 2:5–11, Paul discusses the case of someone who has caused us much grief. He points out that any punishment brought upon the offender "by the majority" is sufficient. Our task as individuals is this: "You ought to forgive and comfort him, so that he will not be overwhelmed by excessive sorrow" (v. 6). When psychologically assaulted by the prodigal, our natural psychological responses are grief and anger. It can be very difficult to set aside our personal pain and remember that here too is a child of God suffering enormously.

Similarly, while we sometimes have to take hard actions against the prodigal, such as evicting him from the home, we should not harden our hearts. In fact, regardless of what we have to do because of his actions, we will affirm our love of this person. This is a stipulation in all of scripture, but was precisely the life and message of Jesus. Contrary to some depictions, Jesus was not at all "meek and lowly," nor was he some passive scholar wandering a little corner of the earth. He was human, experiencing all the emotions and experiences of any human. Yet, one thing never varied. His message ever and always was Love. If we are to walk in Jesus's path, that has to be our message also.[4] The second way we experience the pain of the prodigal is physically. Surely we don't bear any physical wounds, and that's part of the problem. Someone can point to a row of stiches on your arm and say, "Boy, I bet that hurt." The pain is visible. The physical pain of dealing with prodigals most often is not visible, but is nonetheless real. In particular I have in mind the immediate degree of stress prodigals cause. We are accustomed to thinking of stress as a psychological phenomenon, but that is only half of the story. It leads to very real physical effects.

Stress involves our internal "fight or flight" perception. When a threat is perceived, the body releases a flood of hormones—adrenaline and cortisol—which rouse the body for action. For example, if you see that you've headed for an unavoidable auto accident, stress signals parts of your body in how to react—turn, slam on the brakes, and so forth. All of this happens in a split second. That is the good role of stress. But no one can keep this up. To continue the car analogy, it would be like running your car flat out until it's out of gas and oil. It will break down into a useless lump. Stress in dealing with the repeated behavior of prodigals just plain wears our engine down.

4. The Beatitudes in Matthew 5–6 are sometimes called Jesus's lessons in how to love.

While immediate reactions to stress are normally short-lived, and some even beneficial (applying the brakes in an impending auto accident), long-term exposure becomes a cruel punishment with clear physical effects. Chronic stress disrupts nearly every system in the body. Common effects include the inability to wind down or sleep, whirling thoughts, elevated blood pressure, hives, and headaches.

While psychological and physical pain appear to be immediate consequences when dealing with prodigals, beyond doubt spiritual pain also enters the equation. The primary form of this is when we question our own upbringing of the prodigal. As I mentioned earlier, we see a pattern in prodigals that their own guilt or shame forces them to drift away from the church. Frequently the parents will hear statements like "Church is so boring" or "It doesn't mean or do anything for me." These are, to a large degree, "cover-up" statements so they won't have to confront their personal spiritual state. But for the parents it operates in a different way: "I brought my son/daughter up in the church. I tried to do all the right things. What did I do wrong?" Remind yourself that your prodigal child made the choices, not you. Nor are you responsible for those choices. We are all imperfect parents, to be sure, and that does not guarantee perfect children. Only Jesus can bear the weight of the sins of others; we can't.

Make no mistake about it—this is spiritual pain. How many of us lie awake, ransacking our memories for answers? This person—child, spouse, friend—grew up in the faith, perhaps even participated in all the sacraments. Did it all amount to nothing for them, just some required show or superficial ritual? Maybe they did all the right things, but never really entered into saving grace. And, worse yet, was it something we did that caused them to turn away? Unless our hearts have shriveled to a hard, calloused nugget, these are the questions that torment and bewilder us. That daughter of mine. She used to sing "Jesus Loves Me" in a way that rocked the church. Or my son. He is out with friends every weekend, comes home late, hasn't gotten up for church in ages. Or my spouse, who always has something more or better to do than talk about his faith. His religion might be the football game and a bottle of beer. Hers might be those out-of-town trips or that brunch time with girlfriends. Where are the vows that once seemed to mean the world to them? And what can we do, or how should we act?

The second spiritual torment for parents or spouses of prodigals can come from living in the community of faith itself. Most faith communities take seriously Jesus's teaching in Matthew 25:34–36 to feed the hungry, care for the sick, provide comfort and visitation—even to those in prison. But there are also many congregations pervasive with a sense of moral superiority. They don't know how to comfort the needy among them. They are those whom Moses called a "stiff-necked" people, incapable of bending before the commands of God or the pain of others. And such a faith community, with its coldness of sympathy, can cause great pain for parents and spouses of prodigals. They may not be excommunicated, but they are ostracized. People look askance at them. Something is not quite right, after all, to produce a prodigal child or spouse. Furthermore, we who have prodigal children or spouses may feel increasingly uncomfortable among others in church. They all seem to have such perfect lives. They don't, of course, but often that is our perception. The second kind of spiritual pain, then, is this intense sense of loneliness and displacement in the very body where you should be most comfortable.

It seems hard, having faith when everything seems to be going all wrong. Faith is the conviction that God is in control. Faith avows that God knows your situation and has answers for it. Faith asserts that God's promises are true. Faith takes work.

Believers often look at Hebrews 11 as the great pantheon of heroes of faith. Here they all stand: Abel, Enoch, Noah, Abraham . . . Here are the giants. Sometimes, perhaps, we feel the best we can do is sweep up the litter after all the gawking visitors have left the gallery. But we do have to read the chapter to its bitter end. Here we find people who died for their faith in ignominy. They were tortured, abandoned, whipped, imprisoned, and forgotten. Yet they too have their rightful place in the gallery of heroes.

What we miss with an exclusive look at chapter 11, however, is the groundwork upon which each of these heroes stands. The first stage of a three-part foundation lies in the eternal nature of Christ. As John taught, and as is emphasized here, Jesus was "in the beginning," at the Incarnation, and will be at the resurrection and his eternal reign. Second, the author of Hebrews established that Christ is the absolute and for all time sacrifice for our transgression. Third, because Jesus has now won this spiritual victory, the author calls us to perseverance. That is the basis of our faith.

In verses 19–39 of chapter 10, then, the author challenges us to the hardest tasks of modern life—to have faith in God and to persevere through adversity. That is not like human nature. We want speedy results and instant answers. It is not naturally in us to "draw near to God with a sincere heart in full assurance of faith" (10:22). We want to fix it ourselves or get someone who can. Nobody but God can bend the heart, mind, and soul of the prodigal back to him. Faith is not without its reward, however. Consider these words of Jeremiah:

> This is what the Lord says:
> "Restrain your voice from weeping
> and your eyes from tears,
> for your work will be rewarded," declares the Lord.
> "They will return from the land of the enemy.
> So there is hope for your future," declares the Lord.
> "Your children will return to their own land." (31:16–17)

Furthermore, Jesus's words of comfort given to his disciples most certainly extend to his modern disciples: "Do not let you hearts be troubled. Trust in God; trust also in me" (John 14:1).

Our understanding of prodigals often ends with seeing them as children or spouses who squander former values, traditions, and relationships to meet some personal or psychological craving. The fundamentals of drug and alcohol addiction that I have outlined in the foregoing pages are symptomatic of a wider variety of addiction and prodigality. Squandering (the root meaning for prodigal) of traditional values and relationships to meet some personal or psychological craving manifests itself in many ways. I would like to look briefly at two of these—cultural and self-gratification—as examples.

Culture is particularly addictive because it attracts us in two ways. To understand the first of these, we have to understand that culture measures human worth in terms of success. Its addictive property is to achieve more and more success, for in cultural measurement there is always another plateau. Are you worth three billion dollars? Well, Jones down the street is worth seven billion. Therefore you are less successful than he. But wait, there's a cure. Maybe if you spent ninety hours a week at the office instead of a paltry seventy, you could generate another half billion or so. The scenario reminds me of hamsters on their running wheels.

I exaggerate, but the fact remains that our culture confronts us with a full blitz attack of the worldly image of success and it is easy to get addicted to it. When God created Adam and Eve, he called them good. He didn't provide them with tanning booths, Estée Lauder makeup, and Rogaine. Their beauty lay in who they were—the very image of God. But now we're caught in another image and it's worldly success, whether it's having more of the latest toys or whether it's the constant vying to work more and longer hours to increase income.

Such actions, and they are addictions, create prodigals in direct proportion. Our church is a mere block away. Yesterday evening a construction crew moved in to dig up and reinforce the parking lot. Of course I had to join a few neighbors and watch the heavy machinery gobble up and spit out the old asphalt. One worker nearby was edging the old asphalt bed with a shovel. Sweat was flying with the dirt clods. It was after 8 p.m. during our hottest summer on record. I asked him how the summer had been going. "Great," he said. "I've been working eighty-five to ninety hours a week. Steady." Assuming he didn't work on Sunday, I quickly calculated, that's about fifteen hours a day.

I am sitting at my desk the next morning. I usually start writing by 6–6:30 a.m. I can hear the heavy equipment roaring at the church a block away.

I appreciate hard work as much as the next person, but I couldn't help wondering what one loses by working hard for that many hours. And he certainly isn't alone. I know countless people, and occasionally I have had to do this myself, who put in a brutally long day, eat a quick supper, then retire to the office, behind a closed door, to work a few more hours. Some of us do it because circumstances force us to; some do it in response to the never-ending urge to get ahead. The point here is not to condemn people whose jobs entail many hours; rather, it is to pose this question: Whom do we serve? If the labor is simply to satisfy a social image of success, to acquire more money or goods, or to gratify the urge for ever more and ever bigger, then we have signals that things are amiss. If that labor requires more time away from the family, intrudes upon religious and spiritual traditions, and leaves a spouse as sole caretaker (and lonely at that) of the family, then we have signs that the individual is prodigal from their responsibilities. Thus, we have the why, the reason for, and then the effect.

A similar form of addiction and consequent prodigality occurs with self-gratification. In this case it isn't a cultural image of success that governs the behavior, but rather an overwhelming desire to meet our own desires. In *The Great Divorce*, C. S. Lewis unleashed his most electrifying and devastating attacks against the insistence upon personal rights that typifies the modern age. Here a group of ghostly characters from Greasy Town are escorted to the far fringes of heaven and invited by angelic creatures to go further in. Most of them won't make that step. One ghost vehemently insists upon his "rights" and can't conceive of subordinating himself to any other authority. Another ghost conceives of himself as a good actor, not realizing how foolish his vaporous appearance is to the heavenly beings. Only a very few are willing to give up themselves and enter the gates of heaven. Those who insist upon their rights return on the bus to Greasy Town, which becomes everlasting hell.

One term for what Lewis describes is selfishness. If a person insists upon having it his or her way, at the expense of relations with others, the person may be said to live in a prodigal state. The addiction here is "I want it." The prodigality stands in the form of "I don't care what you say." The danger of selfishness lies in the damage it causes to the parent or spouse. They live in a state of belittlement, as if they don't count or are not respected. Furthermore, they feel they have lost *someone* to *something*. They feel abandoned.

A second form of addictive behavior to self-gratification involves illicit or immoral activities. We have already seen the effects of the former in drug and alcohol addictions. A more recent and ever expanding problem occurs in gambling and pornography addictions. In their worst forms they result in damage to the family living expenses by squandering large sums in the lottery or casinos in anticipation of the elusive jackpot someone else always seems to get. Given the odds, you might be better served flushing your money down the toilet. You'd save on gas. Pornography, similarly, has so invaded our lives as to be only a click away. Increasingly it is destructive of home life and an emerging cause for divorce. After all, it's hard for the wife who has put on five pounds having children to compete with the glossy bodies her husband views on the Internet. By being unfaithful to his marriage, he is a prodigal.

Having examined these forms of prodigal behavior, and the ensuing pain they cause, it would be remiss not to consider several responses. No matter how much the prodigal hurts us, and no matter how painful the actions we have to take (the case of addiction to pornography, for example, clearly meets the biblical grounds for divorce), the first response, always and even through pain, is to love the prodigal. Emotions are scarred, cross words spoken, but nonetheless we love that person. We do so for two reasons. First, to love one another is the great biblical commandment. But second, love elevates above the situation into an emotional and spiritual wholeness whereby we gain the confidence that we are acting in Christ.

Second, in our battle with pain, we do well to use a twofold approach— accept the reality and recognize the pain. If we place the blocking defenses of denial about ourselves, we erect a false comfort. Stress accumulates in direct proportion to denial. It takes a lot of hard mental work to deny the evidence of a real problem. Ultimately we try to deny our own pain. In *Parents With Broken Hearts*, William L. Coleman wisely counsels that "We aren't monsters because we become angry. Loss and brokenness are normally accompanied by anger. We have lost something that broke our hearts. Anger can be a healthy expression."[5] The reality is that someone dear to us has caused us great pain through prodigal behavior. I am human, and therefore have emotional needs in confrontation with that pain.

The third topic is also paired. Nearly all counselors of parents and spouses of prodigals will advise them, at some point, to forgive both the prodigal and ourselves. We forgive the prodigal on clear biblical grounds. We have on the one hand the parabolic father receiving his prodigal son back with wide-flung, forgiving arms. On the other hand we have Jesus on the cross, with his wide-flung, forgiving arms open to all of us. That is a gift, and one we can give away to others. This takes some work, for in all honesty forgiveness toward someone who has caused deep pain is hard. But forgiveness is also liberating. When we forgive someone we hand him over to the forgiving Savior. Something of our load is lifted. We don't have to keep probing for causes, that often fruitless pursuit when we look for someone or something to blame. That doesn't exonerate us from all responsibility, of course, but it does deliver us into the knowledge that the Lord who has gifted us with forgiveness also offers it to our prodigal.

Fourth, don't make empty threats. Prodigals become master manipulators. They can find repeated excuses for repeated wrong behavior. They make promises they know they won't or can't keep. If a daughter has stolen from you to support her drug habit, you can't just threaten to report her to the police, you have to do it. If a son steals your credit card and goes through $1,000 of cocaine in one night, you have to report the fraud. They have to bear the consequences of their prodigal behavior, not you. Otherwise, we are complicit in their very prodigality. Similarly, we can't coerce or force a prodigal into our traditional sets of values. As Henri J. M. Nouwen writes in *The Return of the Prodigal Son*, comparing God to the prodigal's father, "As Father, he wants his children to be free, free to love. That freedom includes the possibility of their leaving home, going to a 'distant country,' and losing everything." Nouwen adds, "As Father, the only authority he claims for himself is the authority of compassion."[6] Even as we listen to the lies and manipulations of the prodigal, we know we can do

5. Coleman, *Parents With Broken Hearts*, 67.

6. Nouwen, *The Return of the Prodigal Son*, 95.

little to change the essential heart and soul and mind and strength of that person. Only God, the master of souls and hearts and minds and strength, can do that. Ultimately, we don't give our prodigals up to the world, but to the compassionate authority of God.

This is a matter of setting boundaries. The prodigal has to realize that we stand firm on our values and principles, and that we are not going to become enablers of the wrongful activity. This process also includes positive ultimatums. It is thoroughly legitimate for parents to say to an addicted child, "You're going into long-term rehab or you will be locked out of our house." Furthermore, it is legitimate for a spouse to say, "You're going into counseling for pornography addiction or I'm talking to a lawyer about divorce." All of us need boundaries, not just for our own protection but also against the invasive wrong behavior of others.

Finally, remember that the biblical prodigal came back. Jesus does not tell us all that passed through the father's mind in the years of his son's absence. The son squandered everything, even lying down for the evening in a bed of pig filth. But what incredible pain must have filled the father's mind as he wondered where his son slept that night. His only consolation is ours also. What we see when we look at that teacher from Nazareth, the one miraculously God and man, is not just the blood from thorns and nails, nor the agony of the wounds squeezing his life out like an iron fist, but the veil of tears as he joins in the agony of the world, suffering with us who suffer.

There's a terrible paradox and I don't know anyone besides Jesus who has solved it. We are overjoyed the prodigal has returned. We want to show him or her the fullness of our love and forgiveness. We don't want to live under a cloud. At the same time, we recognize the pain that we have endured and we want to protect against further damage. Counseling, medical intervention, spiritual intercession—they all help, but I'm not sure that any one alone is the final answer.

I do know, however, that a very strange spiritual phenomenon operates in such instances. It's sort of a mathematical equation: forgiveness + time = peace. Forgiveness has its own interior dynamics. We ourselves desperately need forgiveness. Forgiveness, furthermore, is always an act that flows from God and through humanity. Therefore, we are required to forgive since God forgives us.

This important pattern repeats throughout scripture, but especially in the New Testament, in the words of Jesus, who enacted our forgiveness. The fulcrum appears in Matthew 6:14–15, where Jesus says, "For if you

forgive men when they sin against you, your heavenly Father will also forgive you. But if you do not forgive men their sins, your Father will not
forgive your sins." Similar instances occur throughout the Gospels. But
they don't stop there, for to the early church it was a radically new way of
living, quite different from the revenge-driven Romans and Jews. Thus in
Colossians 3:12–13 we read:

> Therefore, as God's chosen people, holy and dearly loved, clothe
> yourselves with compassion, kindness, humility, gentleness and
> patience. Bear with each other and forgive whatever grievances you
> may have against one another. Forgive as the Lord forgave you.

Forgiveness is a necessary and ongoing action of the spiritual life, including
the pain caused by prodigals. But, remember our cautions. Forgiveness is
not an act by which we simply leave ourselves vulnerable. Why? Because
healing is required, and healing takes time. And so we come to the second
part of the equation.

It is often pointed out that Jesus exercises his healing powers in three
ways: immediately, at a word, command, or touch; over time as in a gradual
healing; and not in our time but in eternity. Nearly always, in situations
where we are dealing with prodigals, that healing and restoration occur
over a period of time. This is understandable where a lot of pain has occurred. The greatest dangers of reunions with prodigals collapsing are 1)
expecting perfection from them right now; 2) expecting that all relationships will be perfect; 3) expecting never to have to confront the ongoing
reality of the pain. Healing from prodigality takes time. That pain has been
in the forefront of our consciousness for a long time. It will take quite as
long to eddy back and let newer, pleasanter memories enter in.

And that contributes to the sum of the equation. Let me explain that
with a final example.

Several years ago, while preparing to write a book on Attention Deficit
Hyperactivity Disorder, I interviewed approximately thirty college students
who had been diagnosed with the disorder. The selection age was deliber-
ate since these students were old enough to have an adult understanding
of ADHD and yet young enough to remember the effects of it when they
were growing up. One interview in particular remains in my mind. For our
purposes, I'll identify her by a fictional name, but one that somehow seems
to me to capture her personality.

Elise, a college senior, was one of those naturally attractive and per-
sonable people with whom one immediately feels comfortable. She was so

quick to smile and so calm and articulate in her responses that it was difficult to imagine the tangled and painful path of her youth.

One would think Elise had an advantage. Her father, after all, was a highly regarded psychiatrist, and it is true that he detected signs of his daughter's distress early in high school. He referred her to a colleague, who prescribed the antidepressant Prozac. It seemed a reasonable choice. But then suddenly and without apparent reason, Elise's moods would swing down like a plane falling from the sky.

Elise formed her own opinions. She fought taking medication. In her own words, she "wanted to be normal." Indeed, that seems to be the heartfelt plea of every adolescent. At best, Elise took her medicines when she remembered, or when she cared to, which created a dizzying roller coaster of chemical processes in her brain. Finally she gave it all up to do whatever felt right to her.

I was amazed by how calmly she talked to me about it. I wondered if it hurt her. But her deep brown eyes never left mine. Her voice was strong. This was not the first time I had heard such things. I believed her. Perhaps sensing that, she didn't hesitate.

"My academics finally just fell apart," she said. "I think teachers just passed me along for my parents' sake. I couldn't seem to ever finish a project. I'd write maybe a page in study hall, then forget to finish it when I got home."

"Did you turn it in?" I asked.

"Oh, sure. But I always had this panic the next morning. Like, 'Oh, the report is due. And I only have one page written.'"

Elise didn't so much give up as she rebelled. There were more exciting things to do than one page of a ten-page theme. Her entire lifestyle changed dramatically. With the "help" of some new friends, she discovered a grunge shop. Her expensive wardrobe lay tossed aside in a closet. She adopted the whole lifestyle—piercings, a tattoo—seemingly overnight.

"I imagine your parents were a bit dismayed," I said.

For the first time she averted her glance and paused. "I don't know how I would have made it without them," she said. "Even at my worst, they loved me and stood by me."

"What do you mean by 'my worst'?"

"The whole scene that follows that lifestyle. When you start to rebel, you get caught up in it. Alcohol, drugs, sex." She stated it flatly, without evasion. It was part of the reality.

"What happened?"

"Somehow I did really want to go to college," Elise said. "I was excited about it. In my freshman year, though, I just couldn't manage the work. I was miserable. I wanted to drop out."

Elise realized that she needed help, and she knew that medication would be necessary to be "normal." She submitted to psychological testing, which did reveal ADHD. She has now been placed on medication and engages in therapy to shape order in her formerly ragged life.

One would never believe that Elise who sat before me now was the same person as the one who sat before a therapist four years earlier. Then the therapist saw a young woman with pierced eyebrows, a dumbbell piercing in her tongue, spiral multicolored hair, and the black, spiked collar at her neck. I wonder what the therapist would think, looking at this poised and beautiful young woman who sat before me on an autumn morning.

The difference in apparel and appearance would be most notable. But that anyone could observe. Sometimes it is all that anyone does observe. Surely the difference in body language is pronounced. With the untreated ADHD, Elise fidgeted, paced, couldn't maintain eye contact. Now she sits calmly, hands folded in her lap, and a winsome smile that also touched her lively eyes. The therapist would have likely shaken her head slightly looking at Elise's high school transcripts against her I.Q. scores. Now Elise doesn't mention her college grades until I ask her, and then almost shyly tells me she has a straight A average, but is a little concerned about getting into medical school because her ADHD has prevented her from getting involved in many extra-curricular activities.

What the therapist wouldn't have heard were two things that played like music in my heart. The first was her comment about her parents during her prodigal years: "I don't know how I would have made it without them. Even at my worst, they loved me and stood by me." Her second comment was how, after those years of turmoil, she had discovered Jesus again and made him the center of her life.

I don't have her exact words written down in my notes. How could I? God had honored his promises. We call that God's promise to those suffering the pain of prodigal loved ones. We might not experience it in our lifetime, but there will come a time when their lives will be drawn from north, south, east, and west to be centered once again in Jesus Christ.

Chapter Eight

The Pain of Memories

SOMETIMES ONE CAN, FOR a short time, blot out the pain of buried memories. One almost comes to believe that the memories aren't there anymore, curling like a dragon in the recesses of the brain. Then they come lurching out of their cave again, spewing fire, dragging their scales over a ruined thing we called joy.

The Bible largely omits intimate details of the atrocities that humans visit upon their fellow humans. It doesn't have to do so. The Bible has a one word accounting for all of them: sin. Such a short word to hold so much. Its brevity and overuse gives it a sort of numbing sensation, like an analgesic. Oh, that again. Get over it.

But we can't. Sin forms our heart nature no matter how hard we try to walk in the path of Christ. The detours are wide; the main path narrow. When Solomon told us in Proverbs 4:27, "Do not swerve to the right or to the left," he knew that those side paths were full of trouble. Yet, we daily tickle our toe over the line for a hint of the wayward experience.

I'm talking about the best of us. There are some a few yards down that side path of self-gratification, and others so far down they have forgotten about the main path altogether. These people, these men and women, are moral monsters. They no longer, if ever they did, comprehend the meaning of sin. Their reason for living is to gratify their impulses. They become enraged when thwarted. In their morally deranged minds they inflict all sorts of gross evil upon the innocent and unsuspecting.

When do we have abuse? It seems to me that it occurs any time an action upon us is undeserved and unwanted. That action may be a physical one; it may also be one directed at a person's psychological, spiritual, or intellectual wholeness. In short, abuse is any violation of the order God has created. If Psalm 139 tells us that we are fearfully and wonderfully made, abusers do fearful things with God's wonders. Some are afraid to open a lid to their memories at all, for fear that the bad things will come squirming out. They pile rocks on that lid, and try to live only in the present.

I am not a professional with some psychology degree, certainly not one with vast clinical understanding. My experience is one of listening and reflection. The study of painful memories and the healing of memories has provoked intense and often conflicting debate. Both Christian and non-Christian professionals have weighed in based on their clinical experience. Two of the better studies that I have examined are *The Wounded Heart*, by Dan B. Allender, and *Healing the Child Within*, by Charles L. Whitfield, MD. While such professional expertise is always valuable, and while those dealing with painful memories may profit from therapy, our purpose here is different. First, we want to observe the reality of the pain in the Christian life, and second, as in the pattern of other chapters, we want to see if there are scriptural responses to it.

When I knew her as a student in college, I had no doubt that Heather Gemmen would become a writer. Even then she had what I call "the writer's eye," that peculiar ability to match the prose with craft and care to the subject discussed. Nor was I surprised that Heather went on to become a very successful author and editor of children's books. Yet, nothing prepared me for her book *Startling Beauty: My Journey from Rape to Restoration*. Nothing prepared Heather for it either. Out of one of the worst violations of personal shalom, Heather crafted a poignant testimony that is both graceful and grace-full.

Heather, her husband, and their two children had moved to an inner-city community, purposefully intending to live and worship there as the body of Christ. It was not easy—the all night noise, the being stared at, the break-in just a few months after moving there. To Heather, the situation seemed unrelentingly hopeless and pathetic. Yet, in time she observed a richness in the community disproportionate to the material poverty. In time, the everyday patterns and rhythms of life seemed endowed with their peculiar beauty. Reconciliation began to occur in their local, multiracial church. Here the members all embraced under one banner: children of God. In time the Gemmens adjusted. They called the neighborhood home.

And then everything—everything—changed. Here are Heather's words:

> You chuckled as you sat at the edge of the bed, acting as though you
> had a right to be there. You touched my hair gently, as if your other

hand did not threaten me with a knife. "You gonna like this, baby."
Your breath reeked of beer, and your words fell on me like vomit.
At first I resisted your touches by slapping your hands and moving
away any way I could, but that only increased your pleasure.[1]

Her children were sleeping. Her husband was out. She was alone with the
rapist holding a knife to her throat: "Perhaps the agony would have been
too much for me if I hadn't discovered a place in me where the Comforter
dwelt."[2]

But how can the Comforter deal with the aftermath? One can't erase
the memory like a blackboard. It lies right under the surface and no matter
how hard one rubs the stark letters keep coming through: Raped. Abused.
Tormented. Complete violation.

Then everything seemed to turn topsy turvy. Heather, who had been
trying with her husband to get pregnant, suddenly discovered that she was
indeed pregnant. By the rapist. How, she wondered, can one possibly love
the child growing in the womb, when you hate the father for the act that
created it? Yet even after her beautiful daughter, Rachael Maria Gemmen,
was born, the memory of the past kept its hard nails deep in her mind:
"Rape leaves no room for beauty."[3]

But Heather added:

> But I, for one, have gained more than I have lost. I have been startled
> by beauty in places it doesn't belong. I see it on a bloodied cross, and
> bitterness loses its power. I see it on the face of the man who keeps
> his vows to me, and fear releases its grip. I see it in the graceful dance
> of a child who was so unwanted, and hope revives its song.[4]

What I appreciate about Heather Gemmen's accounting is the fact that she
confronts the ugliness and horror of the event, including all of the emotions in dealing with it. But the darkness of the event doesn't own her. The
beauty of the accounting is that she recognizes and makes room for beauty.
I am reminded of Joseph's response to his fearful brothers: "You intended to
harm me, but God intended it for good" (Gen 50:20).

The pain of memories occurs in two ways. One is for things others
have done to us. The other is for things we have done to ourselves. But this
fact is central to either—each occurs through a betrayal of trust.

1. Gemmen, *Startling Beauty*, 58.
2. Ibid., 59.
3. Ibid., 223.
4. Ibid., 221.

Shalom is a frequently used word in Christian circles today, understood to mean "peace," or "the peace of God." In its Hebrew etymology, however, the word carries richer implications than a greeting. Specifically, it carries the connotation of "my well-being is in God." Those things done to us or that we have done to ourselves that bring pain to our memories do so because they violate our well-being in God. They should not happen to us. They rupture some covenant of peace and well-being.

The question is, then, what does one do about them? And most particularly in the spiritual sense. How does one restore shalom?

I do not use the word *victim* very readily. In fact, I am quite impatient with its use since it now appears to cover everything from pure evil to a bad hair job. When words, an action, or language lodge in persons' memories in such a way as to cause pain and harm, those persons are victims. Power has been used against them. They neither wanted nor can scarcely tolerate this acid infecting their lives. Power can protect; it also can, and too often does, harm and destroy. Power can be, and too often is, an infliction on innocence, an overstepping of boundaries, a forced entering where the door says CLOSED.

Here is what God knows, and what we tend to lose sight of. We find it in the earliest part of creation. When God shaped Adam there really was no Adam at first. The living concept was still in God's creative mind. It was sort of like a team of engineers and designers who shape the clay design for a new car. Except that the design will become a reality only after years of work. In a sense, when God formed Adam he was still that clay model. Adam was "dust of the ground" until God "breathed into his nostrils the breath of life" (Gen 2:7). At that very moment Adam did not become a new car off the production line, battery charged and gas tank full. He became a living soul.

Any unwanted violation of a person's innocence is a violation of that person's soul before God. That's why the memory hurts so much. That person has been robbed of an essential self. In its place stalk fear and shame and, yes, even guilt. One of the most common effects of childhood abuse, after all, is the thought that I must have done something really bad to deserve this. That feeling isn't simply left behind when childhood ends. The point of this is that effective healing of violation becomes a matter of the soul. The victim needs spiritual healing, along with physical and emotional.

This could very well be a long and complicated process, for which, once again, I believe the services of a competent and specialized therapist are called for. It also, however, requires actions that we alone can do for ourselves. Those can be terribly difficult, especially when they require liberation through forgiveness.

I sometimes cringe at the popular slogan "Forgive and forget." I can do that if someone overcharges me a dollar and I'm five miles down the road. But when someone has willfully violated your trust, it can be one of the hardest actions in the world. Try as I might—and frankly I haven't found it in me yet to try very hard—I have not been able to forgive the man who murdered my niece and grandniece. When the glare of his cruel eyes enters my mind, I try with all my strength to shut it out. Forgive me, but I have only once prayed for his soul on death row. I try to live a Christ-like life; that I am not Christ is all too clear to me each day.

Why is it so hard? Because I have to get close to him spiritually to pray for him. And I don't want to.

In fact, sometimes I preach a whole lot better than I do. Sarah (not her real name) sat in the back left corner in four classes of mine. Not only was she as smart as a cracker barrel, but she had a grin that split as wide as an early sunrise. Somehow that narrow band of braces sparkled like jewels in her smile. If all I knew of Sarah were her perfect test scores and her sly humor, I would merely enjoy her presence as another bright student in another class. I also happened to be her academic advisor for four years, a role that involves a lot of talking about hopes and dreams, future careers and past occupations.

Sarah volunteered that she had grown up on a hardscrabble sand farm of forty acres. In time it leaked out that her father, a hard-working and harder-boiled man, worked her like a man on that farm, and never recognized her as a person. I never inquired about the details, but I did know that her father's treatment left Sarah in a world of anguish and self-doubt. It had skewered her view of herself and her view of God. Nonetheless, she was a spiritual seeker, always open to talking about such matters.

I believe it was sometime in Sarah's junior year when I suggested that she tell her father the things she held against him and tell him that she forgave him for it.

"I think you have to do it for yourself," I said. "To put it behind you in your own mind."

"I don't think I'm ready for that," she said.

Suddenly this wasn't the intelligent young woman who sparkled in the classroom, who often handed me poems of such crystalline beauty that I couldn't find a single word of advice to give her. I simply marveled over them. But right now her long hair fell over her bent face and she didn't want to look at me.

"I understand," I said. "And it certainly wouldn't be easy, or it wouldn't be important. But right now those memories have a major hold on you, and I would hate to see you carry them too far into the future. I would like you to release them."

She shook her head, not in denial but with great sadness. "What good would it do?" she asked. "It wouldn't change him."

"We don't know that," I agreed. "But it would change you."

That was the last time we brought the subject up that year. But in her senior year, she returned in the fall and stopped by my office.

"I did what you said," she announced.

"What I suggested," I corrected.

"I'm not sure if it changed my father. But he did listen. And I do feel better that he knows how I feel. I never dared tell him anything."

Interesting. With her academic record Sarah could have gotten scholarships at virtually any graduate school she wanted. I heard from her two years later. She was joyfully managing an organic farm. "It's in my blood," she wrote.

Forgiving someone who has harmed us can be the hardest thing in the world. Why? First, we have to deal with our anger. This shouldn't have happened. The rapist had no right to violate Heather Gemmen. She had every right to be angry at him. Furthermore, there could not and should not be reconciliation between the two. He merits punishment for his action; she deserves to see him punished.

In his landmark book *Forgive and Forget*, Lewis B. Smedes writes about people who simply do not care whether they are forgiven or not. It seems, he points out, to deepen the wound: "When someone hurts us meanly, we want him to suffer too. We expect this clod to pay his dues; we want him to grovel a little. The old-fashioned word for what we want is repentance."[5] Instead, we are left with our pain. But, Smedes argues, there is another way to look at it: "We need to forgive the unrepentant for our own sake."[6]

Second, forgiveness is hard because the violation incurs fear. Something has been destroyed within; that sense of shalom or well-being lies shattered like shards of a broken mirror. You can't go out to the mall and buy a new one. And you can't glue that old self back together again. Always

5. Smedes, *Forgive and Forget*, 89.
6. Ibid., 95.

there is that sense of when might it happen again. Again, Smedes offers a keen insight here: "Only a free person can choose to live with an uneven score. Only free people can choose to start over with someone who has hurt them. Only a free person can live with accounts unsettled. Only a free person can heal the memory of hurt and hate."[7] This is exactly what the victim wants—to be free of the oppressive memory and fear.

Finally, consider this third thing about how hard it is to forgive, but how very important it is to do so. Only through forgiveness come healing and redemptive wholeness. In a sense it is a game of Truth or Consequences, or then again it is a story that you have to read to the final chapter to understand. It is a love story. It is a horror story. It is a tale of awful betrayal and steadfast faithfulness. Many call it the greatest story ever told. Why? Because it is also the story of each one of us.

When Jesus entered Jerusalem for the final days of his life, he did so in a blaze of power. He commandeered the temple in the name of his father; he healed the blind and lame; the next day Jesus preached in the presence of the chief priests, he told parables, he foretold the end of time. What a week!

Then he was alone. The chill dew of Gethsemane sank into his flesh. He walked in sorrow, his heart troubled. He prayed. But of human comfort, he was abandoned.

Only a few of the faithful ones gathered near the cross. I wonder what they expected to see. What they did see was a thoroughly human man die a human death. I suspect that they did not expect to hear these words: "Father, forgive them, for they do not know what they are doing" (Luke 23:34).

Forgive who, though? Forgive us—you and me.

This was the redemptive act for all who repent and seek forgiveness. These words are the foundation on which the pillars of the Christian church rest. These words put us at a hard place. To the Colossians Paul wrote: "Forgive as the Lord forgave you" (3:13).

But I can't, I might say. The pain is too hard, the wounds too deep. Even so. Jesus spoke the words as he was dying. Even earlier, however, Jesus had made a point of these words. One of the cardinal statements of the "Lord's Prayer," is "forgive us our debts, as we also have forgiven our debtors" (Matt 6:12). Immediately following the prayer, Jesus elaborates upon this petition: "For if you forgive men when they sin against you, your heavenly Father will also forgive you. But if you do not forgive men their sins, your Father will not forgive your sins" (Matt 6:14–15).

7. Ibid., 181.

It's easy, I suppose, to forgive someone who has committed some minor trespass against you and asks for your forgiveness. But we can't be Pollyannas before the horror and pain that occur when our shalom is shattered by someone else, particularly someone who evidences not a shred of remorse or pretends that nothing really happened.

With these moral monsters we have to proceed carefully, for they are dangerous. Their abuse cannot be tolerated. It's easy to say, but necessary: we are obligated to get away from them or report them to the police for our own safety—even if it's someone we love. But forgiveness is a spiritual act. If the perpetrator is indeed repentant, so much the better. But generally forgiveness is an act of spiritual healing of memories that are bruised and broken. As Heather Gemmen noted, we rely on the deep warmth of the Comforter even at life's most harrowing moments.

Chapter Nine

"Why Doesn't God Just Make It Go Away?"

Omnipotence and Pain

I HAD VISITED MY doctor for a very minor surgical procedure. As he prepared the site, I was wondering if the problem really required this response. After all, I thought, at my age I can live with a great many imperfections and anomalies. We chatted, the doctor and I, as we usually do. Often our talk turns to theology, since besides being a physician of eminent skill, he is also a priest.

I watched as he flipped out the scalpel, and in a few deft strokes removed the offending anomaly.

"You know," I said, "that looked so easy I bet I could do it myself."

He laughed and said, "Maybe, except for a four-letter word involved."

"What's that?"

"Pain," he replied.

Indeed. Pain is the four-letter word we hate to speak. Pain raises questions and admits to few answers. Pain throws our lives askew. Pain hurts.

Perhaps the greatest challenge to Christian thinking when it comes to the experience of pain is the virtually incomprehensible doctrine of God's omnipotence. We confess, jointly as the Christian church, that God is omnipotent. Many of our central beliefs hinge on that confession. By it we believe that God created the heavens and earth and all that is within them. By it we believe that Jesus defeated the power of evil on the cross. By it we believe that Jesus will return again and destroy evil once and for all. It is our pivotal confession.

Yet, when we apply it practically to ourselves, we sometimes find the confession coming up a bit short. If God is on my side, why do I feel so powerless? And, especially, when I suffer pain why can't or doesn't God just make it go away?

Then we stand perplexed, scratching our puzzled heads. We founder in the gap between God's mysterious power that locked stars into perfect synchronicity in the heavens and our little spinning world of pain. How do we bridge the gap? What answers come forth?

The Human Perspective

The first task is to sort through some popular but biblically errant answers to the issue. They may be based upon correct assumptions, but come to wrong conclusions. The two following steps summarize the basic conflict, but notice that one is from biblical revelation and the other from a human perspective that can't know God fully.

1) If God created all things good (Gen 1:10, 12, 18, 21, 25, 31), including humanity in the very image of God (1:27), then God himself is fully good. The proposition may be reversed. There is no evil in him; therefore, the work of his hands cannot contain any evil.

Consider this analogy, fragile though it is. During a Michigan winter the grass lies dull and dormant as a Narnian winter landscape. But when the spring rains come, that same grass grows a deep emerald green, plush as velvet. It is in the nature of the grass to do so. Were the grass to come up some spring a bright, incandescent pink, as reported by a weatherman, we could only hold one of two conclusions. First, there were some primary defect in the grass itself, or, second, there were a primary visual defect in the weatherman's observation.

But God's goodness, if we are to trust the Bible at all, is his essential nature. He neither contains nor can countenance anything that is not good. Just as the color pink is against the nature of grass, so too evil or wrong is against the nature of God. Being naturally green, grass can't be pink; being by nature good, God cannot do or be evil.

2) Now we turn that biblical revelation to human perception. If God were good, he could choose to make us all happy. It follows, doesn't it? Even the empiricist philosophers, who wanted little or nothing to do with God, declared that the chief end of humanity was happiness. But, as those reading this book know, we are not all happy.

Facing such conflicts, suffering, and unhappiness, or what we call here pain, one might come to one of four conclusions. These are worth mentioning not just for some philosophical argument, nor to say that we hold them all simultaneously, nor yet to say that they are part of the Christian understanding of pain. Rather, I see these conclusions arising from very real human emotions, shared by Christians and non-Christians alike when enduring pain.

The first conclusion deriving from the fact that we suffer pain or unhappiness is not that God is not good. Remember that God is not God unless he is good. That goodness embodies all absolutes we experience—order, justice, beauty, and so forth. Moreover, that goodness embodies the very physical laws by which we daily exist. Mars hasn't collided with Jupiter. One plus one still equals two. An apple still falls to the ground. Scientists may have discovered such orderly truths over time, but God created them. So we really can't claim any of this nonsense about a fickle God, a God who likes to inflict pain, or a God who doesn't care. In fact, the only sensible conclusion to many, then, is that there is no God, at all.

Here is the logic of the atheist. 1) If God is good, our lives ought to be good. 2) But our lives aren't good because we suffer pain. 3) Therefore, there is no God.

The conclusion isn't nearly so sensible as the atheist camp believes, however. Many other writers have ably and clearly demonstrated the necessary (philosophers call it "warranted") proofs for the existence of God. Our concern is with God and our suffering. If someone abolishes an absolute standard of order and good, which we call God, then life is a mere chaos, humanity is without meaning, and our pain is inescapable. The best that can be said is that when you die you are freed from it all. Seen in such a way, atheism is one of the hardest beliefs to hold to. Why? First, because it cannot account for order and goodness apart from random accident. Second, because it is a belief system without hope, condemned to a few years of painful existence. Abandon God and one abandons not only hope, but also joy.

In a second conclusion, people may claim that God, while orderly and all powerful, just doesn't care about our happiness at all. God is an uncaring, cosmic power broker, but not a God with feelings and concern about our welfare. This view shades into contemporary ideas that there may be some power out there (answering to a dozen or more different names) but we alone are responsible for our happiness. Therefore, we have the freedom, some would say the right, to do whatever we want as long as it feels good or makes us happy.

Such a view, and it is quite common as we are all aware, presents two major problems. And they can't be resolved within the conclusion itself.

The first is the Genesis 1:26 problem: "Then God said, 'Let us make man in our image, in our likeness.'" Sometimes people erroneously ascribe this simply to physical appearance, or to ruling authority (humanity over creation). But there is every evidence that it speaks to the total spiritual, intellectual, and emotional character of humanity. God communed (the word means "share in common") with this humanity. They were happy together in a good world. God disciplined Adam and Eve when they disobeyed him. God is not some sort of remote satellite out there, but a living, emotional being deeply invested in the world and humanity he has made.

Furthermore, this conclusion doesn't just make a mockery of the crucifixion, it obliterates its personal and theological significance. Everything hinges on this fact: "God so loved the world that he gave his one and only Son, that whoever believes in him shall not perish but have eternal life" (John 3:16). If anything, the Bible is the story of love. Humans love because God first loved us. Notice the progression in John 15. Jesus says, "As the Father has loved me, so have I loved you" (9). Here we have a chain of love from God through Jesus to humans. But the chain doesn't stop there, for Jesus adds, "Love each other as I have loved you" (12). On this side of Eden, of course, we can't love purely and the love we have is often tinctured with selfish and sinful emotions. But the testimony of a loving, emotional God couldn't be clearer.

The third conclusion arises from the fact that we humans presume that we have a right to happiness. It is in fact a part of our emotional makeup, guided by that rich interplay of biochemistry by which God formed us. As a former runner, I can only remember, but never again experience, that pure elation when, after a mile or two, endorphins flood the brain. And we can all remember or experience those times of laughter with friends. Because of these very times, we might come to believe that this is the chief end of life, that we have a right to happiness.

That claim, however, is as fragile as happiness itself. We know this by experience. The new bride, still rejoicing in her marriage, is diagnosed with breast cancer. That son for whom we had such high hopes with his countless gifts and talents has wasted his dreams and addled his brain with cocaine addiction. That spouse walks out the door after ten years of marriage because she doesn't think she's "in love anymore" and has to be apart "to find myself." And she never comes back.

This is the reality of our human nature. Sometimes it seems that for every honest and upright servant of God, there are ten people with morals lower than pond scum who appear happier. Part of the problem is that we can't really define happiness anyway. If you want some amusing reading, try the definitions in any dictionary. For that matter, try *happy* also. My point is simple; happiness has little real meaning in our daily vocabulary or in our Christian vocabulary. Yet, everyone seems to want it.

Granted, happiness, however inadequately defined, seems to us better than sorrow or pain. But Christians have to come up with a better understanding. We talk about solace, comfort, and joy.

The final conclusion that could be made from the initial conflict, then, is that God is not all powerful over suffering. Instead, pain is like a horrible virus unleashed upon the world. And it's out of control, infecting us one by one without remedy.

The difference between this common conclusion and the others is that it assumes that there is some kind of divine being but he is supremely uninterested in the affairs of humanity. It marks many contemporary Eastern religions—Buddhism, Hinduism, Zoroastrianism, and others—and is an attitude, if not a religion, among many modern Americans. But why would anyone want to hold this view? Why would someone want to claim that God is not all-powerful over suffering and thereby keep him at a distance? Basically, it's the safe way out. It is easier and safer to avoid the issue, especially when this final conclusion boils down to something like this: it is either God's fault or ours. If God is not all-powerful over all things, including pain, then we have no right to name him God. Then the story of God's appearances to Moses is a hoax. There is no "I Am That I Am," nor any Lord of the Ten Laws of Love on the mountaintop. Christian theology tumbles like a pair of loaded dice down a long, dark hole.

By the grace of God, however, there is a different way to look at the issue altogether.

Omnipotence and Grace

If we are to understand God's omnipotence, we have to understand that it works in two ways—universally and personally. By universal we mean God's creative and sustaining power over all things. Something like this may have been in David's mind when he proclaimed, "O Lord, our Lord, how majestic is your name in all the earth" (Ps 8:1). As we saw earlier, evidence of God's supreme power is seen in the very order of the universe. And God sustains this order moment by moment.

The power of God's universal omnipotence is amply testified to in scripture. God created heaven and earth "out of nothing." He needed no other authority than himself. Each act of creation follows immediately upon "God said." No discussion. No conferences. God said it and it was done.

In Revelation, we see that God will create a new heaven and earth. After the raging of battle, after the great chorus of the redeemed, heaven stands open. Aboard a white horse (picture the dazzling brightness!) sat a rider called "Faithful and True." The great rider, who has enacted the final, just, and necessary victory over evil, has done so by the word of God alone—just as Jesus turned back Satan in the wilderness temptation (Luke 4:1–13). In Revelation that word of God is called a "sharp sword" (Rev 19:15). It issues from the mouth of the rider. It is irresistible, all-powerful, and immediate. What the rider says, happens, exactly as in creation. And who is this rider? He has his name written on his robe and thigh: "king of kings and lord of lords" (Rev 19:16). The God who created is also the God who renews at the last battle.

On the one hand, then, we see that God's omnipotence includes his creative and sustaining actions throughout the universe. In the future resurrection, God will create a new heaven and earth. This is our common view of God's omnipotence—the all-powerful ruler whose majesty we can scarcely understand—but it is only part of the story, for bracketed between these events is the Ascension.

In an Ascension Day sermon, Scott Hoezee, Director of the Center for Excellence in Preaching at Calvin Theological Seminary, focuses upon Psalm 47 and its "audacious" claim that here on Mount Zion the very Lord of the universe reigns. It is the equivalent of our audacious claim that Jesus is Lord. "But," Hoezee points out, "Jesus cannot be Lord kind of, sort of, here and there, now and again, or depending on your point-of-view."[1] Yes, it's a strange kind of lordship to human perspective:

> The church doesn't carry a gun. We don't have divisions of tanks. We don't have that kind of clout or power. We're not even as popular as the average shopping mall most weeks. We're like Mount Zion of old: little pin-pricks dotting the landscape of a much bigger world. Worse, it's a world whose headlines almost every day seem calculated to challenge the idea that any kind of good, loving God is in charge of things.[2]

1. Hoezee, "How We See Things," 4.
2. Ibid., 5.

Why do we make such outrageous claims? Because the Lord who came to earth in human form, and that human form was resurrected from the dead and ascended to heaven, Jesus exists neither in the grave nor in heaven alone. Jesus is present with us, even as he is, at once, Lord of heaven. That is the audacious faith we claim.

Omnipotence is both universal and personal. Omnipotence is not only the quality of God whose power is so great that he seems infinitely remote and beyond our understanding. It is also the action of a very personal God who loves us deeply and cares about our welfare in ways we will never be able to comprehend fully. Here lies the truly amazing grace of God's omnipotence: That almighty God truly loves us, with a love that aches it is so rich, to the uttermost of his power and in perfect accord with his eternal plan for us.

This miracle claim of all Christianity rests upon solid scriptural testimony. One of my favorite Old Testament passages comes from 2 Chronicles 32, where Hezekiah and the Israelite army face the vast force of the Assyrian king, Sennacherib. To his men Hezekiah said: "Do not be afraid or discouraged because of the king of Assyria and the vast army with him, for there is a greater power with us than with him" (7). Which power? That of Almighty God who hears the prayer and responds. In this case, God sent one angel who annihilated Sennacherib's entire force.

The Old Testament is replete with examples of God's almighty power in response to his beloved people's needs and prayers. He made the sun go backward and the moon stand still. He parted rivers and brought rain to dry land. But the New Testament emphasizes God's intervention in the needs of his people through the person of Jesus. Jesus, in the miracle of the Incarnation, was fully divine and fully human. As the divine Son of God he stood all powerful over sin, suffering, and death.

One day John the Baptist sent two of his disciples to inquire of Jesus: "Are you the one who was to come, or should we expect someone else?" (Luke 7:18). Remember Jesus's reply?

> So he replied to the messengers, "Go back and report to John what you have seen and heard: The blind receive sight, the lame walk, those who have leprosy are cured, the deaf hear, the dead are raised, and the good news is preached to the poor. Blessed is the man who does not fall away on account of me." (Luke 7:22–23)

One way Jesus exercised his omnipotence as the Son of God, then, was to work with miraculous compassion and power over pain.

As a fully human person Jesus demonstrated two other central qualities of God's all-powerful love for his people. First, he cared deeply for those whom society didn't care about at all. In Jewish society women and children just didn't count for much. But they counted with Jesus. He played with little, dirty, snot-nosed children. He blessed a prostitute and she became his faithful follower.

Not only did Jesus care deeply for others, however, but he suffered as no one else was able to for others. The fundamental truth is that Jesus bore the penalty for our sin, our pain, and our suffering and bestows on us a whole new title. It is not just John, or Beth, or Daniel, or Patricia. It is "Child of God."

This exorbitant claim gave courage to the small, struggling first-century church, despite all its persecution. Paul wrote in 1 Corinthians, "For the message of the cross is foolishness to those who are perishing, but to us who are being saved it is the power of God" (1:18). Again, in Ephesians 1:19, Paul wrote of Jesus's "incomparably great power for us who believe." He adds that "that power is like the working of his mighty strength." Amazing! Jesus gives us the very power he himself holds as Son of God. Yes, you are a Child of God. You never, ever, suffer alone.

When our last child vacated her bedroom, we turned it into a sitting room for Pat. All these years I have had my nicely paneled study, walls lined with bookshelves, plenty of floor space to stack books and folders.

It is, I suppose, a professional necessity for me. But her own private space is a spiritual necessity for Pat. Every morning she heads there, as the sun spills gold through the trees and lays it at her feet. A room full of light, good for reflection, devotions, and quiet. On this day, nothing went quite as usual.

During a recent protracted crisis in our family that just didn't seem to end and seemed instead to worsen every day, Pat found herself in that believer's state of having difficulty focusing her thoughts in prayer. Frustrated by the lack of connection she felt with God and lacking the peace she so desired in this time of crisis, Pat simply made one small plea: Lord, show me some sign that you hear me.

To help start her prayers, she dialed our church's prayer line, where the extensive congregational needs are updated every morning. Unless the heavily used line is busy, the recording always comes on after one ring.

Four rings went by. Obviously she had the wrong number. Pat hung up and got the prayer line on the first ring, as usual. Quickly Pat jotted new information down in her prayer journal. The suffering that afflicts spiritual brothers and sisters of ours! People we have known for years. Several people battling cancer. Many with other diseases, broken bones, discomfort. Still pleading in the back of her mind for one small sign, Pat began to pray for others, as she usually did.

Suddenly the phone rang.

"Did you call me?" the voice asked.

Pat apologized and explained that she was trying to call the church prayer line.

"I'm handicapped," the voice said, "and I can't get to the phone too quick. But I don't think the Lord ever has accidents."

The woman on the phone went on to explain that since her mobility was limited she had become one of the "prayer warriors" for her own church. Then, "Is there anything I can pray for you?"

With a great outpouring, Pat was able to tell of the grief burdening her.

"I meet every Wednesday morning with some women at the church," said the voice. "May I share your needs with them to pray over?"

Pat quickly agreed. Both of us have committed ourselves to being open and honest about our need for prayer. We don't believe in hiding pain or trying to cover it up.

Then the voice said, "May I pray for you now?" And for the next few moments she bathed Pat in the love of Jesus.

The Lord doesn't ever have accidents. We may feel lonely, but we are not abandoned. We may feel pressed down, but he will lift us up. The psalmist cried out,

> Where does my help come from?
> My help comes from the Lord,
> the Maker of heaven and earth.
> (Ps 121:1)

He would not have cried out in such a way unless he was absolutely certain that the Maker of heaven and earth would hear him. So too, we pray with certainty. We don't know how, or just when, but God hears us. And as he hears us nothing is just usual. There are no accidents with God.

Picture this.

Life begins as a path opening up before you. At first, of course, you have no idea you are upon it. You are held by others, fed by others, fully dependent upon others even to survive.

Some time later, after you learn to take steps, you begin to understand that you are walking, and that it is you who is walking. This is called knowledge. You learn about yourself, your hopes and goals. Still, at this point your life path is very sheltered. Decisions are made for you.

If each day on this path represents so many miles you must walk, in perfect parallel to the number of hours that pass, this is the garden stage. The spring trees are full of blossoms. Flowers turn toward the sun near meadows of green. When the rain comes, it seems to fall gently. Life is new every morning, the road festooned with multicolored ribbons of new flowers and blooming shrubs.

Some time later, you are called to duties and obligations. You have tasks to do, some pleasant and enriching, others demanding. It is like those summer days when you labor hard and the sweat rolls down stinging into your eyes, and the sun is hot and brassy in the sky.

You earn a greater sense of this path called life. You learn that it is not infinite, despite all your childhood dreams. Life is not a playground game nor a tent pitched in the backyard. The game might be a struggle; the tent a house that needs too much work on too little income. In fact, sometimes you might wonder just what end there is to this path at all.

Perhaps, as you step forward day by day, you acquire a greater awareness of others walking beside you. Indeed, some may have been there but have now walked on ahead of you. Some who were older, some who were younger. Still, others have stepped into their place alongside you. Some you have grown to love deeply; others you wish you could run away from. But you can't. You are only given each day to walk.

At some point too, you may become aware of Another who wants to walk alongside you. Either you have been vaguely aware of his presence all along, or else it strikes you like a sudden white bolt in your understanding. Someone wants to walk alongside you: you know it like a burning within you.

Some people dismiss this. It is simply, they say, a vague desire that I can better meet with very concrete, specific things. Some treat it like a case of indigestion, and just want it to go away. Some pretend it never happened at all. Some give this Presence a name and call it holy. They feel privileged, for the Presence is royalty. The Prince of Peace.

Mountains arise that you must cross, traveling so far each day. When the clouds lower among their peaks, they paint the world gray. Or you might find yourself one morning in an Alpine mountain meadow, bluebonnets rising in bunches from the long grass that waves ocean green in the wind. The sun plays dappled games in a distant lake, birds hooting and shooting through the light.

At such moments, you might hardly be aware of the one beside you. This is his father's world. Peace itself seems to be your bed at night.

On this long, or short, journey that is your life, you may cross desert places. The dry air scorches your lungs; the hot rocks offer no shelter. You wonder, perhaps, if the one beside you has left you. Why not lie down, give up, and wait to die?

You come at last to hills. You hear the sound of water and find pools where water shines in bowls of rock. Your eyes are still sore and your body weak from the desert crossing; it almost seems someone is helping you drink. In a daze now, you realize you must still travel on, through hills, alongside streams, across ancient rocks that seem trodden down by generations and generations. Each footfall is an effort; pain shoots along nerve endings like a daily onslaught.

You hear the sound long before you reach its source—a long, thundering roll of sound that echoes among the hills and rocks. You understand that is where you must go. With each trembling footfall, you realize this strange thing: it is spring time. The vernal blossoms cover trees like pink and white petticoats. Grass on the hills is like velvet. And you seem to feel a hand on your arm now, guiding you along the path.

You are at the top of a cliff, thrust out like a beacon into the ocean, the last of the velvet grass having given way to rock. In the bright afternoon sun you lean forward—and you lean as far as you can because the grip of the one beside you is very tight now—and see waves froth and crash across the black backs of rocks below. When they eddy back they leave sand so bright it sparkles like a path of pure gold.

You can walk no farther. It is the point where mourning and crying and pain must end (Rev 21:1). You stand at the edge of the cliff and watch the sun descend into the western horizon, passing through its glorious glow of colors. Then the sun becomes a bright golden sphere above the darkening ocean, all the water shading to scarlet and purple until both sky and sea seem to disappear into that last, intense brightness, and you discover you are walking again.

Running, rather. Not over some ocean waves that were the end of that world, but on the golden sand, on the velvet grass. You are not facing a sun that is setting, but one that is dawning all around you. For you are in the light, led by the Prince of Peace to an eternal home that you will never leave and a forever story that will never end.

Works Cited

Allender, Dan B. *The Wounded Heart: Help for Adult Victims of Childhood Sexual Abuse.* Colorado Springs: Navpress, 1990.

Arnett, Thomas. "The Valley of the Shadow of Death." In *This Doesn't Feel Like Love: Trusting God When Bad Things Happen,* edited by Roger Lamb, et al., 180–86. Woburn, MA: Discipleship Publications, 1996.

Augustine. *The Confessions of Saint Augustine.* New York: The Modern Library, 1949.

———. *The City of God.* Garden City, NY: Doubleday Image, 1958.

Bisset, Tom. *Good News about Prodigals.* Grand Rapids: Discovery House, 1997.

Brand, Paul, and Philip Yancey. *The Gift of Pain.* Grand Rapids: Zondervan, 1997.

Buttrick, George. *God, Pain, and Evil.* Nashville: Abingdon, 1996.

Carmichael, Mary. "The New War on Pain." *Newsweek,* June 4, 2007, 40–44.

Carney, Glandion, and William Long. *Trusting God Again: Regaining Hope After Disappointment or Loss.* Downers Grove IL: InterVarsity, 1995.

Chittister, D. Joan. "After Great Pain." *Christian Century,* March 22, 2003, 38–44.

Coleman, William. *Parents With Broken Hearts.* Grand Rapids: Revell, 1996.

Donne, John. "Holy Sonnet X." *Poetical Works,* edited by H. J. C. Grierson. New York: Oxford University Press, 1971.

Gemmen, Heather. *Startling Beauty: My Journey from Rape to Reconciliation.* Colorado Springs: Cook, 2004.

Greene-McCreight, Kathryn. "Review of Three Books on Pain." *Christian Century,* April 18, 2006, 39–41.

Hoezee, Scott. "How We See Things—Psalm 47." *Perspectives,* April 2007, 3–6, 27.

Jackson, Marni. *Pain: The Fifth Vital Sign.* New York: Crown, 2002.

Knoll, Woodrow, and Dan Hawkins. *Prodigal People.* Grand Rapids: Kregel, 1995.

Lewis, C. S. *God in the Dock: Essays on Theology and Ethics.* Edited by Walter Hooper. Grand Rapids: Eerdmans, 1977.

———. *A Grief Observed.* New York: Bantam, 1961, 1972.

Menninger, Karl. *Whatever Became of Sin?* New York: Hawthorn, 1973.

Nietzsche, Friedrich. *Thus Spoke Zarathustra.* Translated by Walter Kaufmann. New York: Viking, 1971.

Nouwen, Henri. *The Return of the Prodigal Son.* New York: Doubleday Image, 1994.

Pearcey, Nancey. *Total Truth: Liberating Christianity from its Cultural Captivity.* Wheaton, IL: Crossway, 2004.

Plantinga, Cornelius, Jr. "A Love So Fierce." *The Reformed Journal,* November 1986, 5–6.

—————. *Not the Way It's Supposed to Be: A Breviary on Sin.* Grand Rapids: Eerdmans, 1995.

Ridley, Ruth Ann. "From Chaos to Cosmos: The Perseverance of J.S. Bach." *Christianity and the Arts* (Summer 1999) 7–25.

Schruer, Jack, and Jerry. *Family Fears.* Wheaton, IL: Victor, 1994.

Shakespeare, William. *King John. The Riverside Shakespeare.* Edited by G. Blakemore Evans, et al. New York: Houghton Mifflin, 1996.

Skinner, B. F. *Walden Two.* New York: Macmillan, 1962.

Smedes, Lewis B. *Forgive and Forget: Healing the Hurts We Don't Deserve.* New York: Pocket Books, 1984.

Tennyson, Alfred Lord. *Selected Poetry.* New York: Holt, Rinehart and Winston, 1956.

Urry, Meg. "Dark Energy." *Parade*, May 27, 2007, 4.

Walton-Moss, Benita. *Substance Abuse: Commonly Abused Substances and the Addiction Process.* Brockton, MA: Western Schools, 2008.

Whitfield, Charles L. *Healing the Child Within: Discovery and Recovery for Adult Children of Dysfunctional Families.* Deerfield Beach, FL: Health Communications, 1989.

Wolterstorff, Nicholas. *Lament for a Son.* Grand Rapids: Eerdmans, 1987.

Wright, N. T. *Evil and the Justice of God.* Downers Grove, IL: InterVarsity, 2006.